Advance Praise for *Smart Alliances*

John Harbison and Peter Pekar have assembled a decade of their writings and consulting experience on alliances into a fascinating manual. Direct and comprehensive, their book represents an unusual combination of thoughtful analysis and pragmatic advice.

> — Bruce Kogut, Dr. Felix Zandman Professor of International Management, Wharton School, University of Pennsylvania

As the president of an association that endeavors to provide our membership with practical guidelines for alliances, I found this book to be one of the best guides on the subject—clearly pointing out the successful as well as the unsuccessful routes to higher return on equity through alliances.

> — Charles H. Conner, President, Association for Corporate Growth

Business alliances are a lot like marriages—hard work, high rewards, but complicated and fragile, too. This book will help you pick the right partner, write the prenuptials, manage the relationship, even deal with the in-laws (overprotective parent companies). A triumph of experience over hope.

> — Barry Nalebuff, coauthor of *Co-opetition* and Milton Steinbach Professor at Yale University School of Management

Companies are increasingly looking to strategic alliances and joint ventures to grow shareholder value and expand globally. *Smart Alliances* is the first authoritative guide to forging partnerships and managing them for success. Alliances will greatly impact shareholder value in the future, which is why executives and managers should read this book now.

> — Steven Kotler, President and Chief Executive Officer, Schroder & Co. Inc.

This should prove a valuable guide in an area that is growing rapidly and, in many cases, into uncharted territory.

> — Joseph H. Flom, Senior Partner, Skadden, Arps, Slate, Meagher & Flom LLP

Smart Alliances

SMART

A *Strategy & Business* Book
Booz·Allen & Hamilton

ALLIANCES

A Practical Guide to Repeatable Success

John R. Harbison

Peter Pekar Jr.

Foreword by William F. Stasior

 Jossey-Bass Publishers
San Francisco

Jossey-Bass books and products are available through most bookstores. To contact Jossey-Bass directly, call (888) 378-2537, fax to (800) 605-2665, or visit our website at www.josseybass.com.

Substantial discounts on bulk quantities of Jossey-Bass books are available to corporations, professional associations, and other organizations. For details and discount information, contact the special sales department at Jossey-Bass.

For sales outside the United States, please contact your local Simon & Schuster International Office.

Manufactured in the United States of America.

Library of Congress Cataloging-in-Publication Data

Harbison, John R.
Smart alliances : a practical guide to repeatable success / John
R. Harbison, Peter Pekar Jr. — 1st ed.
p.   cm. — (A Strategy & Business book, Booz, Allen &
Hamilton) (The Jossey-Bass business & management series)
Includes index.
ISBN 0-7879-4326-6
1. Strategic alliances (Business)   I. Pekar, Peter P.   II. Title.
III. Series.   IV. Series: Strategy & Business book.
HD69.S8H373   1998
658'.044—dc21   98-14182

FIRST EDITION
HB Printing   10 9 8 7 6 5 4 3 2 1

The Jossey-Bass
Business & Management Series

This book is dedicated to our families,
especially to our wives, Renata and Michele,
who had to patiently endure our long hours in
research, analyzing, discussing, and writing
to bring this work to fruition; without their
support and belief in our work none of this
would have been possible. And to our
children—Peter, Robert, Erik, Bill, Pat, and
Michele—who gave up precious time to allow
us to complete this endeavor.

Contents

Foreword

For most of this century, Booz·Allen & Hamilton has been working with the world's largest companies and the teams that lead them. Although this period of history has been as furious as it has been fruitful, the topics that now occupy the busy calendars of CEOs and their leadership groups have not changed much from two or more decades ago. Today, as in the past, business leaders are concerned with how to make their companies more competitive while keeping costs in line and competitors at bay. Business leaders today, as in the past, want to create shareholder value, gain market share, and extend their company's capabilities and reach. While the issues confronting today's leaders are the same as in the past, the context in which those issues must be addressed has changed.

Today's business context is more complex than the environment of the past. That is not to say that previous eras were easier than this one. Success in the past—just as now—has never been easy to achieve. But unlike before, businesses today are confronted with a higher level of complexity brought about by globalization, new technologies, rapidly shifting conditions in the marketplace, and competition arising from the most unexpected places. Entire industries—the minicomputer industry, for example—have come into being, reached their apex, and fallen into the abyss of decline in little more than a decade. Others, like the computer mainframe business, which was once almost written off, have come roaring back.

In some industries, focusing on a company's core capabilities and primary business interest is the route to renewed vigor and prolonged health. Other businesses require the ability to be continuously innovative. Some companies, to prosper and grow, have had to reinvent themselves completely. Monsanto, for example, shed itself of its decades-old chemical business to become a bioengineering concern, while Westinghouse, one of America's oldest companies, transformed itself from a company known mostly for its power-generating equipment, including nuclear powerplants, into a media company that renamed itself CBS.

To survive and prosper, some companies have formed linkages with their chief rivals while others have severed linkages with their closest friends. Seen one way, this has been a period of mergers, alliances, and outright acquisitions. Seen another, it has been a period of divestitures, uncouplings, and recouplings. Seen all ways, it has been an era of complexity.

Today's perennial problems, unlike yesterday's, require a host of new, highly individualized solutions. Since the level of complexity is so high, the ability to create cookie-cutter solutions is at an all-time low. As a result, what matters is the ability to analyze problems carefully, quickly, and creatively. What matters is solving problems in fresh and disciplined ways. What matters is the ability to think about a subject while keeping the market in mind. What matters most is creativity.

The aim of *Strategy & Business* books is not to tell business leaders what to think. That would be both presumptuous—even foolhardy—given the rapid rate of change, the diversity of companies' situations, and the personalities of today's business leaders. Rather, the aim is to tell business leaders what to think *about*. The difference between *what to think* and *what to think about* is the difference between a rigid list of thoughts dictated by some font of wisdom, and an agenda set out for discussion. In the current period, the ability to discuss, reason, and argue scenarios and points-of-view beats rigid dictation every time.

Over the last several years, Booz·Allen has spent a lot of time mulling over the corporate agenda. It has done so by interviewing leaders, surveying firms, reviewing its own assignments, and consulting with academics. The contents of this book series—and this book—reflect the contents of the business agenda.

What we have found in our research is that the big concerns over defining values and vision, managing people and risk, adapting to changed markets and new technology, and assessing performance and portfolio mix have only become more important as competition intensifies, the speed of computers multiplies, companies become more complex, and the economy becomes increasingly global.

At the same time, because of external pressures and changing management approaches, new ways of thinking about those concerns have swept through boardrooms and across factory floors with remarkable synchronicity. Some of these shifts reflect radically different orientations; others are wholly pragmatic in nature.

In our own work, we have recently seen the focus of the CEO agenda shift toward growing the top line rather than cutting costs and toward managing the new corporation instead of restructuring the old one. As we see it, three variations on these themes reflect the new agenda for CEOs and their top teams:

Managing for growth
Business process redesign, the next generation
The new organization

It seems clear what has caused CEOs to shift their focus. Many major companies, though not all, have completed the first wave of business process reengineering (BPR) and have thus achieved the first 80 percent or so of cost restructuring. They must now look to revenue growth for the next quantum leap in performance improvement. This situation puts managers in an expansive frame of mind that the rebound in corporate profits over the past several years undoubtedly reinforces.

At the same time, the wave of delayering, restructuring, and reengineering has left many companies in a twilight world between the old and the new. Traditional management processes have been discarded and dismantled; new ones are not always comfortably in place. Learning to manage in the post-restructured world has become a life-and-death priority, which has implications for the CEO's role in shaping a company's core capabilities and critical priorities and in determining which functions to outsource and which to leave in-house.

- *Emerging markets.* Even with Asia's current economic problems, most CEOs look to the emerging markets there and in Latin America (and to a much lesser and potentially myopic extent, eastern Europe) as the keys to future growth. On the one hand, there is the infrastructure boom ($1 trillion by 2000, according to some estimates); on the other, there is an almost infinite potential consumer market as more and more segments of these huge populations enter the market economy. Already, there are about 300 million "consumers" who can purchase power parity in the world's emerging markets. And that number represents only 10 percent or so of the total population of those areas.
- *New products and services.* The ability to sustain innovation in products and services is becoming a principal source of competitive advantage across a broad range of industries.
- *Acquisitions, mergers, alliances, and post-merger integration.* As balance sheets have improved, the number of corporate acquisitions has started to rebound dramatically. In fact, there is even evidence that part of the value liberated by recent acquisitions is being captured by the acquirer's shareholders and not just by those of the acquiree, which has overwhelmingly been the outcome historically. This trend is consistent with our observation that today's acquisitions appear to have a greater fit with the acquirers' core strategies and capabilities than was true in the past.
- *Strengthened "blocking and tackling."* Our clients are placing increased emphasis on the basics in their businesses: enhanced customer care; better marketing and sales force management; and improved, tactical pricing. Much of this change is overdue. Despite the claims of many analysts of BPR, recent rounds of reengineering and restructuring have left many of these basic processes weaker than before.

Relative emphasis among these growth channels necessarily varies. Our own analysis of one hundred companies with an above-average increase in shareholder wealth over the past two decades suggests that expansion in emerging markets is the greatest source of growth; break-out strategies that redefine the basis of competition in mature industries come second; and continuous product innovation and brand building come third. Acquisitions worked less well, with a few notable exceptions.

To capture differentiated growth, CEOs need to foster new and enhanced competencies and attitudes within their organizations. Innovation, for example, has long been viewed as being as much the product of lucky breaks as of a business capability that one can design, upgrade, and manage. As a result, many organizations avoid managing their innovation capability for fear of tampering with creative forces that they do not wholly understand. In fact, as companies such as the Chrysler Corporation and the Sony Corporation have shown, companies can design and manage innovation capability in a number of ways. These include strengthening the business processes associated with understanding markets, planning product lines, managing technology, and developing products or processes; improving measurement systems that track innovation; and developing systematic processes to capture and deploy organizational learning and best practices.

Similarly, to capture the full long-term potential of emerging markets, CEOs will have to move the center of gravity of their organizations, their managerial brain trusts, and their own mind-sets toward these markets—and there is a long way to go. Winning in emerging markets also requires a different type of decision-making process. The pace of change is so fast that traditional planning processes simply do not work. For example, markets that took a decade to develop in the United States and six years in Japan are evolving in less than two years in some parts of China.

What is needed is strategic entrepreneurship, a relatively clear view of long-term objectives, and a strong set of strategic boundaries that can be used to screen opportunities. CEOs also require a highly entrepreneurial approach to creating and exploiting opportunities and shifting between scenarios as they unfold.

Growth also brings uncertainty and more complexity, however, which has implications for how companies must think about risk management. Among the "perennials" on the CEO agenda, we have found that risk management is the issue demanding the most attention.

As CEOs think about growth, their time frames are lengthening. We love to ask clients to estimate their time horizon. Answers vary, depending on the near-term health of their businesses, but strategic focus has moved out to about seven years. On earlier occasions, eighteen months was not unusual. During the last couple of years, our firm has experienced a surge of engagements focused on modeling the relatively distant future and on leading management teams through strategic simulations or sophisticated war games for their industries.

Changing demographics, technology advances, and global shifts have far-reaching implications for competitive boundaries and patterns of demand in virtually every industry. CEOs increasingly view one of their core roles as stimulating their companies' perspectives on what the future will bring. The boldest among them will select a scenario and remold their businesses accordingly.

CEOs have long understood their role in building the corporate vision. Today, this focus is being complemented by a drive to establish and entrench clear corporate values. These are not simply a means to edify the spirit but are vehicles to communicate strategic focus and operating boundaries to all employees. This represents a shift from the focus of most strategists ten year ago.

The breakthrough implies a focus on both vision and communication. The entire organization must understand the company's strategic direction and feel empowered to reach that goal.

A related trend in organizations is renewed interest in the role of the corporate center or core. At a recent symposium at which Booz·Allen partners discussed the most important business issues on the agendas of the firm's clients, we discovered that thirteen of the twenty-five participating partners were working with major companies to retune and redefine the role of the corporate center.

To some degree, that reassessment relates to the need to change management processes to fit the post-restructured corporation. It is also driven by external, competitive pressures, however; the same market pressures that compelled companies to lower costs are forcing them to rethink the integrative logic of their business portfolios.

Much of the thinking in this field comes back to address which businesses belong in the corporate portfolio and how the parent can add value rather than subtract it, as is too frequently the case. In addition to the traditional debate over the most appropriate forms of strategic and financial performance systems, this wave of reexamination is focused on building truly global organizations (in many cases, with traditional "center" functions being distributed geographically), on conceiving and managing strategic alliances and other extended enterprise relationships, and on some of the "softer" forms of added value.

The latter include the inculcation of shared corporate values and identity and the capture and deployment of organizational learning and best practices. Increasingly, corporate added value is more a matter of applying intellectual capital than of sponsoring scale economies in unit costs.

We are also seeing greater top-level attention focused on managing through processes. The wave of restructuring, reengineering, and delayering demands different management approaches than those used in the past. Yet the new approaches have been slow to develop. In a recent analysis that we conducted of twenty-eight "post-reengineered" companies, we found that in most cases, the CEOs and their top management teams were continuing to manage essentially as before. They used the same decision, planning, and control processes and the same management information and reporting systems. Most recognized the disconnection but were uncertain about how to resolve it. The answer lies in taking the following actions:

- Reorienting top executives to manage and enable "processes" rather than organization units
- Explicit reengineering of the decision-making processes involving top management itself, with related changes in authority delegation and style
- Creating new performance management systems that complement the reengineered world and incorporate an ability to learn

In beginning to address these issues, CEOs are also beginning to take more seriously some of the concepts that they nominally embraced over the past several years. The horizontal organization, team-based management, the learning organization, empowerment, and similar concepts have had their place in the executive lexicon for several years. The body language of most CEOs continued to reinforce older, more hierarchical traditions, however. This is now beginning to change as CEOs gain a greater understanding of these ideas and become more sincere in their desire to practice them.

The final element of the new organization relates to the players themselves. Building the management team is always a CEO agenda item. Today, virtually all CEOs with whom we talk say that creating greater entrepreneurship and teamwork among their top one hundred managers is their Number 1 challenge.

There are several drivers behind this renewed focus on the top team. Above all, the pace and volume of change that most corporations face demand that the load be shared; the CEO cannot typically expect to shoulder it alone. Then, too, there is a need to rebuild the social contract between managers and the company. One consequence of restructuring and downsizing has been a unilateral revocation of implied loyalties.

CEOs are exploring various approaches to reengineering their teams, including explicit team-building exercises, adjustments to measurement and rewards systems, and experimentation with such devices as internal "venture funds" designed to stimulate entrepreneurship. We are also seeing a renewed focus on selection, including a willingness to reach outside the home team to enlist the best athletes.

As CEO agendas evolve, the natural question is whether the current focus is correct. In our view, the new agenda is properly directed. Nevertheless, it is almost certain that the next decade will see a sorting of winners from losers at least as significant as the one that occurred during the last two decades. Fewer than half of the Fortune 500 listed twenty years ago are still on the list today, and a fair number of the survivors owe their position to their leviathan scale rather than to stellar performance.

Companies that lost their position failed because they had insufficient insight into their customers' needs and the implications of technology and other trends. In addition, they allowed service bottlenecks and excess costs to accumulate in their delivery systems. As a result, overseas and greenfield competitors were able to outdeliver and undercut them.

In theory, the new CEO agenda will help business leaders avoid similar missteps in the future. It will do this in a number of ways: the concentration on growth and innovation implies improved customer understanding and strengthened value propositions; the second wave of BPR will improve value while keeping costs lean; and the new organization will focus on shared learning, continual improvement, and greater entrepreneurship. Overall, we observe a more concerted attempt by CEOs to understand and position their companies for the future.

In practice, of course, some companies and some CEOs will do better than others. That is the nature of competition. From our vantage point, though, it is clear that the winners will be those CEOs who can integrate the new agenda with their own clear vision while simplifying the execution challenge and inspiring their organizations to perform beyond all expectations.

New York, New York   William F. Stasior
August 1998   Chairman and Chief Executive
                   Booz·Allen & Hamilton

Preface

Both of us began our journey in the world of alliances in the early 1980s. Back then, alliances were few in number and were generally limited in scope. Competition was simpler, and companies did not need to excel in all capabilities in order to compete effectively—one differential capability was often enough. The pace of change in technologies and markets was modest compared with today's activity, and industry boundaries were well defined and generally not global. If you lacked a capability, you either took the time to develop it or you bought it through an acquisition. Shareholders were (relatively) patient and less demanding about profitability and returns. In short, companies in the "good old days" did not require the capabilities that successful alliances produce.

What happened?

As the pace of technological change accelerated, industry boundaries began to blur, and new capabilities were required to be successful in new convergent markets (such as electronic banking). Globalization became the rage. In turn, companies needed new capabilities to defend current positions and take advantage of opportunities. As competition intensified, they found they needed strong capabilities across all business activities. But increasing financial pressures and shortening product-innovation life cycles left managers without the time or resources to fill these capability gaps through internal development. And acquisitions were an expensive way for companies to access specific capabilities beyond those traditional to an industry because they ended up paying for unneeded as well as needed capabilities and often found themselves managing businesses outside their areas of expertise.

As a result of these pressures, the business world has seen an unprecedented surge in alliance activity in all industries and in all situations. Just as the reengineering boom swept the world in the early 1990s, alliances are now seen everywhere as a powerful way to implement strategies and to manage businesses. CEOs are realizing that they cannot cost-cut their way into growth and prosperity, because there is a limit to how much you can grow earnings by improving margins. Clearly, companies need to be competitive in costs, but usually they must access incremental capabilities before they can achieve top-line growth. Alliances are among the solutions for accessing those capabilities. Unfortunately, until recently, most companies were relatively inexperienced in forming and managing alliances, and among those that did have experience, most had little institutional learning taking place to foster future alliances.

In 1988, we got a taste of the emerging importance of alliances when we surveyed the CEOs of the Fortune 500 companies. One hundred and fifty-seven questionnaires (with fifty detailed questions) were returned. Half of them had been filled out by CEOs, presidents, or COOs, and the remainder had been filled out by either the chief strategist of an alliance or by the operating executive in charge of an alliance. The same pattern occurred in 1993 with a survey we sent to the CEOs of the *Business Week* top 1,000 companies. The questionnaire was expanded to fifty-nine questions, and again we received a significant response of 283 questionnaires, again half filled out by top management. These responses reinforced our conviction that alliances were indeed an important topic, given the response rate and the seniority of managers willing to invest time in such a detailed survey. In the period from 1994 to 1996, we surveyed the one thousand largest companies outside the United States with an eighty-nine-question survey and received over one hundred responses. And in 1997, we looked in-depth at the alliance activity of forty selected major companies to learn what they were doing to institutionalize alliance capability.

We asked why they had entered alliances and what they had experienced. We also asked what they wanted to know about alliances, and the response was intriguing. Books and articles on the subject were starting to surface, but the CEOs we talked to found them too anecdotal and not practical enough. These CEOs knew that their companies lacked experience doing alliances and that this contributed to a low success rate, yet they weren't sure how to avoid a painful learning process. One respondent put it succinctly: "If I decided to try playing a round of golf without any experience or lessons, the outcome would be obvious—I'd likely be an embarrassment to those playing with me and I'd be sure to fall short of any possible measure of success other than being alive at the end of the round. The same thing with alliances. In golf, there are plenty of places to go for practical lessons, but in alliances I haven't found anyone with a methodology that makes sense and that goes beyond a series of anecdotes."

With this kind of feedback, and armed with detailed findings from the surveys, we set out to fill that void. We formed an alliance *special interest group* at Booz·Allen & Hamilton, which included consulting partners from every major industry practice and geographic territory— all with experience and expertise in alliances. The group members met monthly by phone to capture the firm's best thinking on the subject. We wrote the *Viewpoint* publication *A Practical Guide to Alliances: Leapfrogging the Learning Curve,* which quickly became a Booz·Allen best-seller (with 18,000 copies distributed, it is now in its third printing). We organized conferences, made presentations, and attracted media coverage. Since then, we have written other *Viewpoint*s on alliances and conducted other surveys, along with our continuing experience helping clients make and manage alliances and building alliance process capability. This book reports on our journey so far, our choices for "Greatest Hits" of the alliance world.

By picking up this book, you share an important interest with those CEOs who responded to our surveys. You may be a newcomer to alliances, or your company may have participated in a few of them. In the latter case, you know how difficult they are to form and manage. In either case, you may want to learn more about the best practices of the most successful companies. Perhaps your company has formed scores of alliances, but learning does not seem to be taking place, and you are looking for a disciplined process to manage these arrangements. Or you may just be curious about the numerous alliances announced prominently in major newspapers and business magazines and on television. Simply, whatever your level of interest, you want to jump the learning curve.

By selecting this book, you are taking a critical step toward broadening your knowledge of the alliance phenomenon. And for that CEO who set out the challenge for us, you may not get a hole-in-one, but your handicap should drop, and you should start shooting more and more pars, as well as an occasional birdie.

Acknowledgments

Many people and companies have contributed ideas, suggestions, and insights to keep our work creative and focused. Although we cannot thank them all here, we would like to single out a few whose insights and creativity at critical stages drove us to question long-held beliefs and moved us to explore new avenues. We are also indebted to Booz·Allen & Hamilton and its steadfast encouragement, enthusiastic support, and consistent funding as we explored our new paradigm.

In particular, we are deeply grateful to our CEO, Bill Stasior, who recognized the emerging importance of the extended enterprise and supported our efforts; Bruce Pasternack, for his support of our initiative in our strategy leadership practice and his concept of the *Centerless Corporation;* Chuck Lucier, chief knowledge officer, for his sponsorship and for *10x Growth;* and Cy Freidheim for his pioneering work on the *Trillion Dollar Enterprise.* All deserve special recognition for their originality and for challenging us to perform rigorous analyses to support our ideas. Thanks also to John's mentors, Frank Varasano and Dan Lewis.

We owe a special debt of gratitude to our global alliance special interest group, which kept us on track and helped pioneer many of strategic alliance concepts. We especially thank our non-U.S. committee members, who endured monthly conference calls at odd hours in their respective countries in order to give our work a truly global perspective. These partners and colleagues include Ian Buchanon (Singapore), Augustin Castano (Argentina), Étienne Deffarges (France), Hugh Dickinson (UK), Viren Doshi (France), Alex Gneisenau (Munich), Ian Godden (UK), Kevin Jones (Tokyo), Gerry Komlofske (China), Lorenzo Larraguibel (Chile), Karchi Lukac (Mexico), Doug Ng (China), Wouter Rosingh (Brazil), Martin Waldenstrom (France), and Lando Zappei (India).

Many partners and industry experts were instrumental in sharing their understanding of strategic alliances and providing valuable insights to case studies. From our industry practices, we would like to thank Gerry Adolph (chemicals), Dan Aks (computers and electronics), Charlie Beever (pharmaceuticals), Dennis Conroy (telecommunications), Kyle Datta (energy), Mitch Diamond (utilities), Scott Gable (consumer products), Tom Hansson (airlines), Marc Powell (computers and electronics), John Rhodes (energy), Matt Rogers (oil and gas), Scott Schulman (entertainment), Steve Silver (computers and electronics), Eric Spiegel (energy), John Treat (energy), and Reggie Van Lee (telecommunications). Our thanks also to Tim Laseter for his work on strategic sourcing and to Jim O'Toole for his work on leadership. Finally, we thank our senior partners, Jack McGrath, Harry Quarls, and others, who helped us take our intellectual capital to clients for real-world testing.

Special thanks to Wouter Rosingh, Artur Ribeiro Neto, Doug Ng, Ian Buchanon, Gerry Komlofske, Kevin Jones, and Alex Gneisenau for writing sections for the chapter on lessons and opportunities across borders.

For contributions to the chapter on governance, we thank our friends at Sidley & Austin, and in particular James Archer; Gregg Kirchhoefer, a partner in the Chicago office of Kirkland & Ellis; and Albert S. Golbert, a partner in Golbert Kimball & Weiner of Los Angeles.

Many of our friends in the academic and professional communities provided helpful suggestions, including Gary Hamel of the London Business School, Michael Yoshino of Harvard University, Kathryn Harrigan of Columbia University, José de la Torre of UCLA, Philip Mirvis of the University of Michigan, Al Rappaport of Northwestern University, and Yves Doz of InSead. We are especially grateful to the Conference Board, our annual alliance conference cosponsors, for insights and support;

Ron Cowin, who has helped us attract a panel of world-class alliance experts each year; Jim Bamford of the *Alliance Analyst* for insights and comments on our work; and Heidi Lorenzen of Business Week and Dominick Attanasio at the National Association of Corporate Directors for suggestions and encouragement of this research.

For her editorial assistance, we thank Renata Harbison, who (as final copyeditor on this book and all of John's published articles) has kept us honest and, we hope, clear in our prose. And thanks to Joel Kurtzman, editor of *Strategy & Business,* for his assistance in bringing this book to fruition.

As important as all this help and guidance has been, it would not have meant anything without the support of the clients who challenged us every day. They provided insight and direction for the research as it unfolded, and they stretched our imaginations by challenging us to be innovative. They questioned our work at every level and provided constructive criticism, testing our findings and methodology in the crucibles of their companies.

Los Angeles, California   John R. Harbison
August 1998   Peter Pekar Jr.

Smart Alliances

Introduction

When it comes to corporate strategic alliances, the numbers speak for themselves. No, not just speak: they fairly shout for attention. Our surveys show that

- Strategic alliances have consistently produced a return on investment of nearly 17 percent among the top two thousand companies in the world for nearly ten years. That is *50 percent more* than the average return on investment that the companies produce overall.
- The twenty-five companies most active in alliances achieved a 17.2 percent return on equity—40 percent more than the average of the Fortune 500. The twenty-five companies least active in alliances lagged the Fortune 500, with an average return on equity of only 10.1 percent.
- Since the early 1990s, the percentage of revenue that the one thousand largest companies in the United States have earned from alliances has more than doubled, to 21 percent in 1997. In 1980, it was less than 2 percent! By 2002, the successful alliance builders expect about 35 percent of their revenue to come from alliances.

Given such results, is it any surprise that strategic alliances are being much more widely embraced? More than 60 percent of chief executives in the United States approve of alliances, compared with 20 percent five years ago (see Exhibit 0.1).

Is it any wonder that alliance activity is surging around the world?

Sources and Purposes

For fifteen years, we have been surveying global alliance activity, recording and analyzing its extraordinary growth. From the responses, we have created a database of more than five hundred companies, involved in more than six thousand alliances. These surveys were augmented by in-depth interviews with top executives; by surveys of alliance activity and

Exhibit 0.1.   Today's CEOs View Alliances Positively

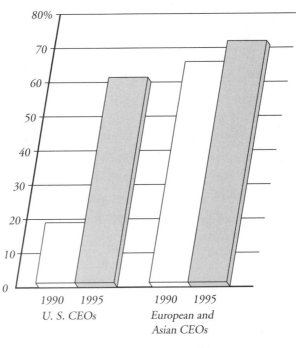

Perceptions of Alliances as Successful

Source: Various Booz·Allen & Hamilton surveys.

attitudes conducted jointly by Booz·Allen & Hamilton, the *Wall Street Journal,* and the *Nihon Keizai Shimbun;* and by our work with corporate clients. In recent years Booz·Allen & Hamilton has also sponsored annual conferences jointly with the Conference Board in New York and in Europe, enhancing our dialogue with senior executives concerning their views on alliance activity.

From this wealth of material, we have created practical, actionable guidelines for managers that go beyond theory and anecdotal discussions. Drawing on the work of the most globally oriented U.S. companies and also the expertise of the European and Asian companies that have moved quickly to build strategic alliances, we convey underlying principles and a clear, disciplined methodology that can help executives thoughtfully consider their alliance strategy.

Our goal is to move all executives who are currently taking an "I Own This!" or "This Piece Is Mine!" perspective to a new understanding of why companies must work together to grow. We also provide a window through which executives in different regions around the world can get a sense of the alliance activity flourishing beyond their boundaries.

Unlike previous books about strategic alliances, this book goes beyond theoretical discussions or studies of a handful of corporate activities, and beyond profiles of one or two large alliances. Our unique database of alliance activity allows us to identify and share factors distinguishing the most successful alliance makers from the pack.

Readers of This Book

This book is intended for all business executives, whatever their level of experience in alliances. It aims to provide a guide for all those who want to create strategic alliances but are uncertain how to go about it, for those who still have reservations about joining forces with others, and for those with considerable alliance experience who want to know what their counterparts around the world are doing.

Business leaders who have taken the lead in forging alliances—including Jack Welch at General Electric, Wisse Dekker at Philips,

James Houghton at Corning, George Fisher at Eastman Kodak, Bill Gates at Microsoft, and Lew Platt at Hewlett-Packard—have little doubt about the importance of strategic alliances for companies traveling the path to global growth. Yet many executives still find alliances disconcerting, a sort of *liaison dangereuse* of the business world. And indeed, a strong and workable alliance is complex to negotiate—far more difficult than an acquisition (see Exhibit 0.2). However, studying what alliances have achieved; what they promise; and how they can be effectively selected, negotiated, and managed can help executives grow more comfortable with alliance strategy. Once they understand that effective alliances are used not to compensate for weaknesses but to create competitive strengths and strategic positions, then they can take the lead in helping their organizations overcome inhibitions about risk taking and resource sharing.

Exhibit 0.2. Strategic Alliances Are More Complex to Negotiate

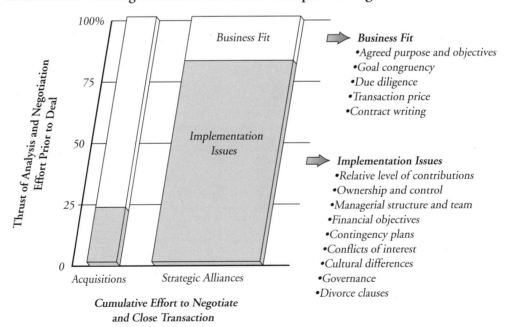

Overview of the Chapters

The eight chapters of *Smart Alliances* move from recognizing alliance opportunities to acting successfully on those opportunities and then to developing the ability to predictably repeat the process, not once but many times.

In Chapter One, we explore the rationale that is driving alliances today. We also define strategic alliances, explore how they differ from other business relationships, and introduce the primary objectives companies typically seek when they form alliances.

The numbers that are creating the momentum behind alliances are revealed in Chapter Two. This chapter also examines the motivational drivers of the leading practitioners of alliances and presents a test you can use to determine whether alliances are a critical priority for your company.

Chapter Three introduces the basic concepts you need to leapfrog the alliance learning curve: several key principles, seven best practices of successful alliances, and seven pitfalls that successful alliances know to avoid.

Four case studies of major alliances are presented in Chapter Four. The stories of Fuji Photo Film and Xerox, Corning and Siemens, Wal-Mart and Cifra, and Hewlett-Packard and Canon reveal many sides of successful alliance practice as it occurs between different types of partners (and competitors) in the real world.

In Chapter Five, we move from examples to the methodology we have derived from our surveys of many existing alliances. We describe in detail our eight-step roadmap to successful alliances and present many more of the best practices we have found.

The lessons U.S. companies can learn from more experienced Asian and European alliance builders and the opportunities that cross-border alliances offer are discussed in Chapter Six, along with essential information about business practices and goals and economic and political realities in the regions of Asia and Latin America.

Chapter Seven addresses broad legal and governance issues—from worst-case scenarios to alliance funding to tax codes—that alliance partners must address, especially when planning and negotiating the alliance.

Finally, the companies that are most successful with alliances have learned the importance of embedding the capability to create alliances in the corporate structure. This step unlocks the secrets of repeatable success. Chapter Eight explores the various ways successful companies are institutionalizing their alliance capability.

The New Key Questions

When should management or corporate directors consider the alliance option? Some warning signals ring loud and clear:

- The company has no alliances at a time when its competitors and its industry do. A company with far fewer alliances than its rivals may also be at competitive disadvantage.
- The company has had a failed alliance or is unhappy with the results of a current alliance.
- The company has a current alliance that is of critical importance but is in disarray. It is time for a tune-up.
- The company has gained some alliance experience, but it is reinventing the wheel with each new alliance. The company enjoys no visible learning from its alliances.
- The company needs more capabilities than it has time or resources to develop.

Few business combinations are inconceivable today. Fierce competitors Microsoft and Netscape formed an alliance in 1997 to standardize future 3-D browser formats. Historical rivals Thomson-CSF of France and GEC-Marconi of Britain created a strategic alliance to offer sonar to the global defense market. In fact, although some alliances are formed by companies in completely unrelated businesses, 55 percent are formed by competitors. Even Bill Gates of Microsoft and Steve Jobs, now back at Apple Computer, have agreed to work together after being bitter rivals for so many years, and Microsoft has made a significant investment in Apple.

How do competitors go forward with alliances? By relying on the vision, rigorous analysis, and careful planning and negotiation of their managers. Why do they do it? Because these companies and their leaders understand that the key question is no longer, Should we form a strategic alliance? but rather:

- What types of arrangements are most appropriate?
- How do we successfully manage these alliances?
- What are we learning from the experiences of ourselves and others?

As we examine the results of our research in the following pages, our numbers raise yet another question, Can you afford to wait? The gap is growing between companies with successful alliances and those less active or less successful. Laggards may wonder, How can we close the gap? How do we acquire the necessary experience?

The methodology presented in this book, the list of best practices culled from the many companies we have studied, and the detailed look at the alliance activities of several corporate giants and at successful alliance activities in Europe and Asia provide detailed, practical answers to these key questions. This book takes you on a journey from recognizing opportunities to repeating success. We are confident that you will find the trip worthwhile.

Chapter 1
Opportunities and Imperatives

It was a brisk November day at the Zhukovsky airfield outside Moscow as Sergei Borisov, a test pilot for the Tupolev Design Bureau, taxied his Tu-144LL supersonic airliner to the end of the runway, nudged his throttles to full thrust, and held his breath as his aircraft took off. The aircraft, refitted with new engines and new avionics, had not been flown in earnest in fifteen years.

As the Tu-144LL, a delta-winged, dropped-nose plane known informally as the Concordsky, gained altitude, Borisov was not the only one holding his breath. So were a handful of U.S. executives watching the test flight at the once-secret airfield. In a remarkable demonstration of how deeply the post–Cold War world had thawed by late 1996, the giants of U.S. aerospace—Boeing, McDonnell-Douglas, Rockwell International, General Electric, and United Technologies—had joined with Tupolev in search of the next generation of supersonic travel.

If a more stirring reminder of glasnost and international alliances were needed, at a welcome party a few months earlier a Red Army band and chorus had greeted the Western visitors to Zhukovsky field with "God Bless America."

What brought these U.S. military contractors to Russia? An understanding that there were skills and experience to be had that would enable them to leap forward—*if* they could find the right alliance. Given

9

the relatively limited deployment and the long flight to modest profitability of the Concorde (developed by British Aerospace and Aerospatiale of France), no single company was prepared to commit the huge resources needed to develop a faster and larger supersonic plane. Only a strategic alliance could come up with a sufficient investment without a bet-the-company exposure.

The seeds of this unlikely alliance were planted in 1993, when U.S. and Russian executives met at the Paris Air Show. The Russians desperately needed capital. Russia's aerospace industry, its military spending generally, and its entire economy, to say nothing of its political environment, were more than a little unsettled. The Americans were looking for a way to jump-start their vision of a day not so far off when a larger, faster successor to the Concorde would be viable. Together they settled on the Tu-144, first ordered by the Soviet government in 1963, brought into service in 1975, but retired in 1978. (One problem with this original aircraft was that its engines were not fuel-efficient enough to permit the long flights that take advantage of supersonic speed.) The Tu-144 would become the Tu-144LL, and "the Tu-144LL describes what the next generation of supersonic aircraft will probably look like," said a senior engineer with the National Aeronautics and Space Administration, which prodded and supported the U.S. companies.

In late 1993, U.S. vice president Al Gore met in Moscow with Russian prime minister Viktor Chernomyrdin, and one item on their agenda was the redevelopment of the Tu-144, the first major cooperative aerospace venture between the two nations. The U.S. companies agreed to put up $10 million in seed money, the Russian government somewhat less. Within weeks, the alliance had taken shape, and U.S. and Russian personnel were sharing what had once been state secrets. The alliance was a sign of the times.

What forces mark these times, and what are the characteristics of the strategic alliances that more and more companies are seeking?

The Rationale for Alliances

Corporate alliances are not new. Westinghouse Electric and Mitsubishi have been allies for seventy years; Chevron and Texaco since 1936; Dow Chemical and Corning for fifty-five years. What *is* new in the 1990s is the accelerating proliferation of strategic alliances, their scope, and how they stand distinctly apart from cartels, keiretsu, joint ventures, and other business relationships. What all this alliance activity reflects is business executives' perception that the corporate world has never appeared as hostile, bewildering, and unstable as it does today.

The New Reality

Three major forces create this unsettling new reality:

- The globalization of markets
- The search for capabilities as technology blurs industry boundaries
- Scarce resources and intensifying competition for markets

When a company scans its environment and assesses its own resources and capabilities, it often discovers—as Boeing, Rockwell, and the other partners in the Tupolev alliance did—a gap between what it would *like* to achieve and what it is realistically *able* to achieve. It confronts the reality that fundamental competitive changes are taking place across the industrial landscape.

The company and its beleaguered executives must contend with the lowered prospects for growth, the accelerating rate of technology deployment, the increasing global competition, the opening of many new markets, and the emergence of new regional trading blocs. Formerly disparate products, markets, and geographic regions are now firmly linked. Competition is no longer confined within a single nation's borders. The company's strategic goals—whether they require gaining a certain market share or achieving a certain competitive position—are often unattainable in the new environment of global competition. Exhibit 1.1, for example, illustrates how U.S. companies' partners in alliances are now spread around the world.

"If you think you can go it alone in today's global economy, you are highly mistaken," Jack Welch, chief executive of General Electric, one of the most active international companies, observed in an interview. As rapid technology shifts and changing markets motivate companies to tailor products and services, management is under pressure to act faster and more shrewdly while using fewer resources. This makes the

Exhibit 1.1.   U.S. Companies' Alliance Partners Spread Around the World

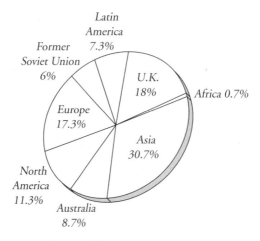

Country of U.S. Partners, 1995

Note: Includes deals signed, alliances waiting approval, and letter of intent alliances.
Source: Securities Data Corporation; Booz·Allen & Hamilton analysis.

identification, protection, and enhancement of core capabilities the key challenge of our time. Absorbing new knowledge and capabilities to strengthen core competencies has become a necessary skill in improving performance in this new environment.

The Example of Oracle Systems

Few companies embrace alliances with more fervor than Oracle Systems, the database software leader. The company has thousands of alliance partners in nearly every facet of its business. "We have been trying to solve some major problems," said Oracle president Ray Lane, in a presentation to the Conference Board in April 1997. "We see an evolving pattern that we are moving away from vertical integration—the process of basically controlling every process involving material and products—to a process of outsourcing and 'virtual corporations.'" Oracle has even adopted new vocabulary to describe its alliance activity: *coopetition* and *complementarity.* "With coopetition you have to adjust your culture to learn to be a partner and a competitor at the same time," Lane said. "To compete and cooperate is a real-time value chain. Things are constantly changing the value chain and you have to accommodate it. Complementarity is quite different. The value chain is well defined. Different competitors have delineated goals. No one has overlap of business scope."

Oracle partners range from its software competitor SAP to accounting firms like Deloitte & Touche. The company divides its alliances into three categories: *industry solution initiatives,* with one exclusive partner; *cooperative application initiatives,* with any company that wants to design a connection to its software programs; and *technology partners,* which number in the thousands. "In the past we were constantly beaten by our competitors because we were so slow in making decisions about platforms or moving software," Lane said. "Now we have earlier access to technology and gain additional critical mass and resources. All of these things become benefits, rather than getting in our way."

The Growth of Capabilities

In the 1980s, a company could rely heavily on mergers and acquisitions; many did and some still do. But a growing number of companies have learned that they need other long-term options. A company might be motivated to negotiate a strategic alliance when, for example, it faces strategic gaps in critical differential capabilities that are too expensive or will take too long to develop internally. An alliance is also attractive when one company wants access to a subset of another's capabilities, but not all the excess baggage that an acquisition might bring. An alliance can also prove the best approach when the desired capability is in the hands of a partner too big to consider seriously as an acquisition.

Through a strategic alliance, companies can select, build, and deploy the critical capabilities that will enable each of them to gain competitive advantage, enhance customer value, and drive markets. Their goal is to focus on the capabilities that they can use to renew their positions constantly. Competitive advantage in capabilities comes from precision tailoring and sharp focus, from using strategic alliances to fill critical capability gaps.

Consider what Ford Motor Company and Mazda Motors have wrought over the decades through a deeply embedded strategic alliance. The companies' first dealings came as early as 1931, when Ford was asked to make a three-wheeled combination motorcycle-truck in Japan for Toyo Cork Kogyo, Mazda's predecessor. In 1969, the companies agreed to a traditional subcontracting arrangement, with Mazda making some parts for Ford.

By the 1970s, Ford and Mazda could see the advantages of a broader alliance. Like General Motors and Chrysler, Ford had failed to develop a strong entry in the growing North American market for small, fuel-efficient cars. So in 1979, Ford took a 25 percent stake in Mazda. Mazda built compact cars for Ford, and Ford was able to leverage its Mazda relationship by arranging for Mazda-designed cars to be built in Taiwan with Mazda-supplied components. In South Korea, Ford and Mazda worked with Kia Motors to develop a subcompact car for the North American market.

Mazda provided more than just small vehicles. Its cutting-edge concepts in design and manufacturing, especially at its highly automated Hofu plant in western Japan, became a center of learning for Ford, which used this expertise to improve its European operations and to build a similar plant in Hermosillo, Mexico. Ford also looked to Mazda for lessons on how to create profitable vehicles for small niches markets, as Mazda did so dramatically with its Miata sports car, introduced in 1989.

From Mazda's perspective, the alliance with Ford solved several large problems. Most dramatically, the alliance offered a path to survival in a crowded field of eleven Japanese automakers. The alliance also promised ready access to the massive North American markets, where Mazda badly lagged its Japanese competitors. (That access, however, has not fulfilled its promise. Despite occasional successes like the Miata, Mazda's North American sales still lag behind those of its major Japanese rivals.) The alliance provided Mazda with deep pockets, and for that reason was strongly encouraged by Mazda's lead banker, Sumitomo. And when the Japanese auto market reeled in the 1980s as a strong yen dented export sales, Ford stepped in once again with an additional investment of $481 million in cash, raising its equity stake to 33 percent. Recently, Ford's executive vice president, Henry D. G. Wallace, became president of Mazda Motors, the first time anyone other than a Japanese has headed a major Japanese industrial company.

The alliance has continued to broaden its reach. Ford and Mazda announced in April 1997 that they would synchronize production cycles of many different vehicles in order to better share platforms, engines, and transmissions. A major area of interest to both companies is Southeast Asia. In Thailand, Ford and Mazda are jointly operating the Auto-Alliance plant, which is expected to produce pickup trucks that will give Ford increased competitiveness in this region where Japanese vehicle manufacturers now hold 90 percent of the market. "We are competitive partners in the best sense of both words," Wallace has said of the alliance.

The best alliances are built on goals for the future, and it is essential that they not be viewed as static arrangements. Just as Ford and Mazda continue to amend and transform their alliance, so must any effective partners find flexible and effective means to respond to their changing know-how needs and emerging critical processes.

Defining Strategic Alliances

Individual companies find many different ways to extend their enterprises through other companies, from conventional sourcing and service arrangements at one extreme to acquisitions and mergers at the other. Exhibit 1.2 illustrates an extended enterprise continuum, in which the vertical axis is a measure of commitment, ranging from traditional, modest transactions up to permanent relationships. The horizontal axis is a measure of ownership, ranging from no linkage up to wholly owned. The term *alliance* can describe a broad range of the relationships that fall within these extremes, from short-term projects, to long-lasting relationships between a supplier and a manufacturer, to broad strategic alliances in which partners tap into and learn from each other's capabilities.

Exhibit 1.2.   Strategic Alliances Are Part of an Extended Enterprise Continuum

STRATEGIC ALLIANCES

Commitment \ Ownership	No Linkage	Shared Information	Shared Resource	Shared Funding	Cross-Equity	Shared Equity	Wholly Owned
Permanent		Outsourcing relationship	For example, RPR and Gencel		For example, Japanese keiretsu	For example, Caltex	Acquisition For example, Ford and Jaguar
Long-term				For example, Tristar (CBS; HBO and Columbia Pictures)	For example, PowerPC (Motorola, IBM, and Apple); For example, Anheuser-Busch and Kirin	For example, J&J and Merck	
Transactional	Annual or multiyear purchase agreement	Distribution agreement	Cross-licensing	R & D program partnerships			
Transactional	Commodity purchase order	Collaborative marketing	Collaborative advertising	Purchase agreement with up-front funding			

Ownership →

Commitment →

Transactional Alliances

Clustered in the lower-left portion of Exhibit 1.2 are various modest relationships, often limited in both duration and scope, that we think of as *transactional alliances:*

- They generally last less than five years.
- The partners do not share critical capabilities.
- The relationship does not involve control and is usually contract driven.
- The partners do not share a common strategy or act in unison; they remain at arm's length.

Among the many forms of transactional alliances are *collaborative advertising* or *marketing, shared distribution,* and *cross-licensing.* The examples abound. A hamburger chain offers children an action figure based on a new Hollywood movie. American Express and Toys-R-Us cooperate on television advertising and promotion, as do Rubbermaid and Home Depot. Nissan sells Volkswagen vehicles in Asia; Volkswagen distributes Nissan cars in Europe. Dreamworks, a new Hollywood studio, and Universal Pictures sign a ten-year agreement: Dreamworks will create nine films, and Universal will put up $1 billion and receive distribution rights outside of the United States, Canada, and South Korea. The deal also gives MCA, which owns Universal, the right to use at the Universal Studios amusement parks whatever animated characters Dreamworks creates. Hoffman-LaRoche will sell Glaxo's Zantac, an antiulcer drug, in the United States. Apparel makers buy cloth made abroad; major automakers buy windshields, brake shoes, and electronics from suppliers; and some computer companies buy CD-ROM drives and modems from other manufacturers.

Strategic Alliances

In this book we focus not on these relatively modest relationships but on the broader, deeper alliances—the middle ground between transactional alliances and acquisitions. These *strategic alliances* have the following distinct characteristics:

- A commitment of at least ten years
- A linkage based on equity or on shared capabilities
- A reciprocal relationship with a shared strategy in common
- An increase in the companies' value in the marketplace, placing pressure on competitors
- A willingness to share and leverage core capabilities

Cytel and Sumitomo Pharmaceuticals worked to develop the next generation of biotechnology drugs. Mitsubishi Electrical and Lucent Technologies plan to jointly develop and manufacture an advanced microchip that will be used in high-definition television. Strikingly, many such alliances are now driven by industry agendas to cross national boundaries (see Exhibit 1.3). Even more strikingly, many of the most

Exhibit 1.3.   Many Alliance Activities Cross Borders

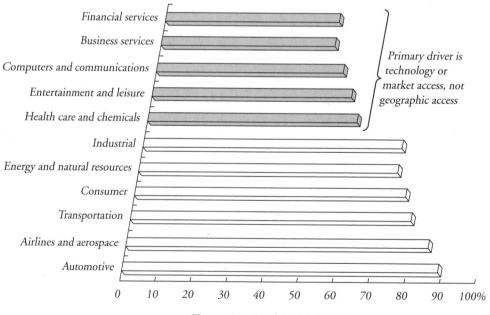

Transactions Involving Multiple Countries

Source: Booz·Allen & Hamilton analysis of worldwide transactions, 1994–1996.

successful strategic alliances, like Hewlett-Packard with Canon and General Motors with Toyota, are between rivals (see Exhibit 1.4).

Facing billions of dollars in development costs, Toshiba of Japan, Siemens of Germany, and International Business Machines of the United States agreed to jointly design a new type of chip, the 256-megabit D-RAM. Roughly fifty engineers from each of the three companies worked side by side at the IBM facility in East Fishkill, New York. All three companies, through sophisticated high-tech communication systems, have access to all data and information generated in the program.

Some strategic alliances involve companies in entirely unrelated industries. Taito, a Japanese sugar producer, teamed with Pfizer, the U.S. pharmaceutical company, to create a pharmaceutical company that competes successfully in the Japanese market. Microsoft formed an alliance

Exhibit 1.4.   Half of Recent Alliances Are Among Competitors

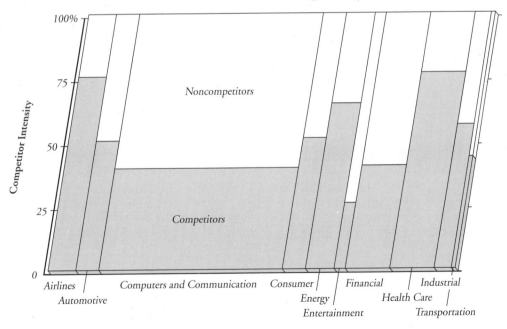

Comparative Proportion of Alliances by Industry

Source: Booz·Allen & Hamilton analysis of 2,000 alliances, 1994–1995.

with NBC, the television division of General Electric, to create MSNBC, a cable television and Internet service (see Exhibit 1.5 for further examples of strategic alliances).

Strategic Alliance Objectives

Partners' objectives in a strategic alliance are different from objectives in a transactional alliance. Here are the typical objectives in a strategic alliance.

• *Risk sharing* (because you can no longer afford the risks of bet-your-company investment opportunities). Eastman Kodak, for example, realized years ago that electronic media and imaging posed long-term threats to its film business. After a series of home-grown initiatives, Kodak's senior management concluded that the company lacked the ca-

Exhibit 1.5.   Recent History Provides a Variety of Alliance Examples

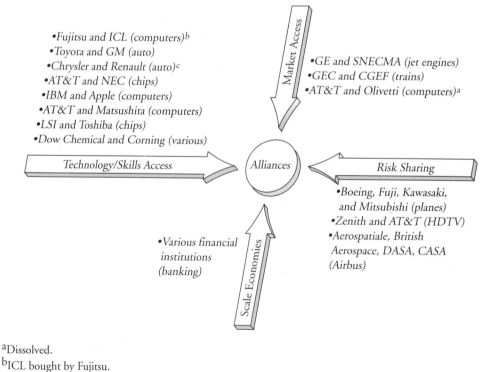

•*Fujitsu and ICL (computers)*[b]
•*Toyota and GM (auto)*
•*Chrysler and Renault (auto)*[c]
•*AT&T and NEC (chips)*
•*IBM and Apple (computers)*
•*AT&T and Matsushita (computers)*
•*LSI and Toshiba (chips)*
•*Dow Chemical and Corning (various)*

Market Access

•*GE and SNECMA (jet engines)*
•*GEC and CGEF (trains)*
•*AT&T and Olivetti (computers)*[a]

Technology/Skills Access   *Alliances*   *Risk Sharing*

•*Boeing, Fuji, Kawasaki, and Mitsubishi (planes)*
•*Zenith and AT&T (HDTV)*
•*Aerospatiale, British Aerospace, DASA, CASA (Airbus)*

•*Various financial institutions (banking)*

Scale Economies

[a]Dissolved.
[b]ICL bought by Fujitsu.
[c]Cancelled.

pabilities and market position to gain customer acceptance of a new film format taking advantage of new technology. Kodak therefore entered into a significant alliance in the early 1990s with its fiercest rival, Fuji Photo Film, and three camera makers, Canon, Minolta, and Nikon. Together these companies invested billions of dollars to create the Advanced Photo System, a technology that allows a person using one camera with a fixed lens to switch back and forth among standard, close-up, and wide-angle pictures. No one company had had the innovation capabilities, the energy, or the money to develop APS alone. Now these alliance partners are licensing the technology to other companies in the photography field.

• *Economies of scale* (because your industry has high fixed costs and you need greater scale to compete globally). Such cost pressures led British Airways and American Airlines to forge an alliance. Two of the world's largest airline computer reservations systems also joined forces to develop new products, cut costs, and improve service: START (a German system owned by Lufthansa, Deutsche Bahn, and TUI) and Amadeus, the world's largest booking system (owned by Air France, Continental Airlines, Iberia, and Lufthansa).

• *Market segment access* (because you lack a basic understanding of customers and applications and you lack the relationships and the infrastructure to distribute your product to customers). Wal-Mart, the largest retailer in the United States, and Cifra, the largest retailer in Mexico, agreed to work as equal partners on various projects in the Mexican market. Petronas, the Malaysian natural gas company, took a 30 percent stake in Engen, a petroleum retailer in South Africa, in order to gain a beachhead in the African market. In addition to access to Engen gas stations in Africa, Petronas hopes to gain a partner for exploration and refining ventures throughout Africa and the Indian Ocean.

• *Technology access* (because you face critical technology gaps, and you cannot afford the time or resources to develop the technology yourself). IBM, Motorola, and Apple Computer joined together to create the PowerPC microprocessor, which created a next-generation alternative to the Microsoft Windows–Intel near-monopoly on personal computer operating systems and microprocessors. Fisher Price, a unit of the toy giant Mattel, teamed with Compaq Computer to develop educational computers aimed at the family market. The project joins Fisher Price software and expertise with children to Compaq hardware and expertise with high technology.

- *Geographic access* (because you are frustrated with the difficulty of penetrating a foreign market where the opportunity is attractive and for which you have a viable product). America's largest brewer, Anheuser-Busch, joined with brewer Kirin of Japan to strengthen each's hold in the other's home markets. News Corporation and Softbank agreed to jointly acquire a 21.4 percent stake in Asahi Broadcasting, a Japanese television network. Similarly, Asia Business News, a satellite broadcaster based in Singapore, teamed up with the Kyodo news agency of Japan and with Jupiter Programming, a Japanese cable-television distribution company, to offer a twenty-four-hour business news program on Japanese television.

- *Handling of funding constraints* (because you are confronting large and ever-increasing development costs). In 1991, Boeing, General Dynamics, and Lockheed joined forces to pursue a Pentagon contract to develop a new, advanced tactical fighter aircraft. It was one of the largest Pentagon contracts ever, expected to generate about $1 billion annually at first and later more than $5 billion annually, and in previous decades these prime aerospace contractors would have tenaciously fought one another for it. But each company had concluded that it alone could not handle the enormous scope of the project. The competition that the alliance beat out was yet another team of former rivals—Northrop, McDonnell-Douglas, and General Electric. Under the agreement, Lockheed is responsible for overall performance, navigation and other avionics, the forward fuselage, and final assembly. Boeing will provide the aft fuselage and install the engines and wings; General Dynamics will provide the center fuselage, weapons bay, landing gear, and tail.

- *Skills leverage* (because you need to access skills or capabilities faster and at a lower cost than internal development permits). Glencore, an international trading company, wanted more expertise in the market for lead, so it took a 15 percent stake in Metaleurop, the world's leading lead producer. Bankers Trust reached an alliance with CIS, a claims-processing company, to offer a processing service to the health care industry. IBM, with an eye on the huge market in Japan for wireless devices, reached an agreement with NTT, the Japanese telecommunications giant. The two companies will jointly develop a "personal handyphone system" that NTT will market in Japan.

• *Value-added barriers to competition* (because you want to strengthen skills and raise the level of competitive intensity for your industry). The Washington Post Company, for example, reached an agreement with a Russian publisher, the Most Group, to produce a Russian version of *Newsweek* magazine. It will mix content prepared locally with content prepared by the Newsweek organization and translated into Russian. Most will sell advertising space to Russian advertisers, and the Washington Post Company will sell space to advertisers worldwide.

Just as they have distinctly broader objectives than transactional alliances, so too do strategic alliances stand apart from *cartels,* which are formed to restrict trade and maintain price structure, and from *keiretsu,* which are designed to maintain uninterrupted vertical sources of supply. The strategic alliance also goes beyond the *joint venture,* historically defined as a new business entity owned by two or more sponsoring companies and sharing resources and skills—and the emphasis is on *owned.* Often cross-border joint ventures join a stronger company with a weaker host company, seeking a way around national or government constraints.

Strategic alliances are typically alliances of equals, linking the core capabilities of each partner to increase value to the customer. A strategic alliance works best when an acquisition is not feasible, when an evolutionary approach is desired, or when each partner recognizes its need to access critical capabilities it is unable to develop by itself. At the heart of every strategic alliance is a focus on selecting, building, and deploying only those capabilities that can truly drive the market. The singular pursuit of building those capabilities is the only thing that ultimately matters. "As long as there is better expertise on the outside, to succeed we must use that," says Thomas Natale, senior vice president for operations at Philips Consumer Electronics (Lewis Jordan, *The Connected Corporation,* 1995). And as we show in the next chapter, a startling number of companies are finding that they need better capabilities and are forging strategic alliances to get them.

Chapter 2
The Momentum Behind Alliances

The numbers alone are startling. More than 20,000 alliances have been formed worldwide in the last two years, and more than 70 percent of them involve some form of equity. In the United States, even though it has lagged behind Europe and Asia in alliance growth, the number of strategic alliances has grown 25 percent annually since 1987, and the United States now accounts for about one-third of the world's alliances. European and Asian companies form 50 percent of the world's alliances (see Exhibit 2.1). The remainder are in Latin America, Africa, and India, where one strong engine of alliance growth is the increased willingness of local companies to work closely with multinational corporations.

As striking as the geographic spread is the range of industries that now embrace alliances. For many years, natural resources and manufacturing were the most intensive sectors for alliance formation. This no longer the case. In the 1990s, alliance formation ranged from health care companies to telecommunications firms, to service industries, and to such traditionally local businesses as electric utilities, funeral homes, and even used-car sales. Although telecommunications, computer hardware and software, biotechnology, and medical services remain the hottest sectors for alliances (accounting for nearly half), the assumption

Exhibit 2.1.   Alliance Numbers Are Surging Worldwide

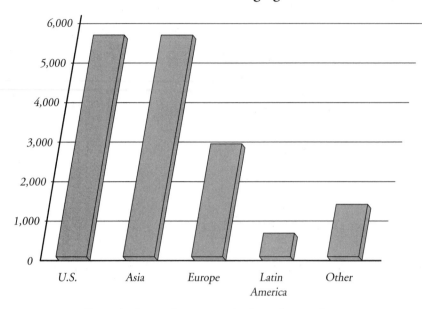

Alliances by Region (January 1994 – September 1995)

Source: Strategic Data Corporation; Booz·Allen & Hamilton analysis.

that alliances belong in the realm of high technology is not accurate. Growth is clearly evident in financial institutions and services, transportation, retailing, and elsewhere (see Exhibit 2.2).

What drives all this alliance activity? The rest of this chapter shows how financial results and other corporate motivators are encouraging many companies to form not one but multiple alliances. We also provide a short questionnaire to help you determine your company's alliance needs and readiness.

Revenue, ROE, and ROI

Again, the numbers tell a striking tale. The percentage of companies' revenue that comes from alliances has been surging. As we pointed out in the Introduction, for example, the percentage of revenue that the one

Exhibit 2.2.   Alliances Are Relevant to All Industries

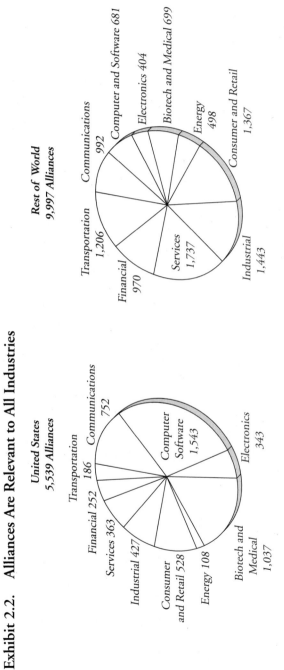

United States
5,539 Alliances

Transportation 186
Communications 752
Financial 252
Services 363
Industrial 427
Consumer and Retail 528
Energy 108
Computer Software 1,543
Electronics 343
Biotech and Medical 1,037

Rest of World
9,997 Alliances

Transportation 1,206
Communications 992
Computer and Software 681
Electronics 404
Biotech and Medical 699
Energy 498
Consumer and Retail 1,367
Industrial 1,443
Services 1,737
Financial 970

ALLIANCES BY INDUSTRY
(January 1994 – September 1995)

Source: Strategic Data Corporation; Booz-Allen & Hamilton analysis.

thousand largest U.S. companies have earned from alliances has more than doubled since the early 1990s (see Exhibit 2.3). In 1995, it was 15 percent; today it is 21 percent, and these companies expect about 35 percent of their revenue to come from alliances in the near future.

More than 90 percent of the executives polled in our most recent survey predicted the percentage of revenue that comes from alliances will continue to grow. At some companies, alliances already contribute far more than the average. Aerospatiale, the French aerospace giant, earns more than 80 percent of its revenue from alliances.

The impact of alliances on the bottom line is just as striking. Recall that according to a survey conducted by the *Alliance Analyst* newsletter, the twenty-five companies most active in alliances achieve a 17.2 percent return on equity (41 percent more than the average ROE of the Fortune 500), whereas the same survey found that the twenty-five companies least active in alliances produced a return on equity of only 10.1 percent (see Exhibit 2.4).

Return on investment was also higher among alliance-oriented companies. Whereas the one thousand largest U.S. companies had an aver-

Exhibit 2.3.   Alliances Are Growing as Sources of Revenue

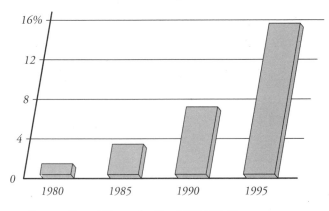

Revenue from Alliances for Top 1,000 U.S. Companies

Source: Data from Columbia University and European Trade Commission (cited in Kathryn Harrigan, *Strategies for Joint Ventures,* Heath, 1985); studies by Booz·Allen & Hamilton, 1983–1987, 1988–1992, 1994–1996.

Exhibit 2.4.   Alliances Result in Higher ROE

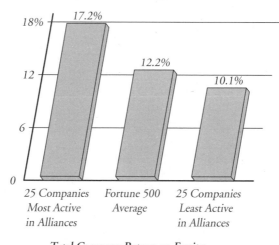

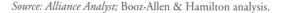

Total Company Return on Equity

Source: *Alliance Analyst;* Booz·Allen & Hamilton analysis.

age return on investment of 10.8 percent, strategic alliances produced a return on investment of nearly 17 percent (see Exhibit 2.5).

Alliance Drivers

Beyond the pure numbers, strategic alliances are gaining prominence because of an evolution in corporate motivators, or *drivers* (see Exhibit 2.6).

In the 1970s, corporate emphasis was on product performance. Alliances generally focused on obtaining access to the latest technology and selling products internationally, but the key selling point was always product performance. In most cases the boundaries between industries were clear-cut, so companies did not need to access broader sets of capabilities. In the 1980s, the emphasis shifted to company position. Each company sought to build its stature within its industry, consolidating position and seeking economies of scale and scope. The 1990s, however, brought dramatic change. As industry lines blurred and markets became global, the emphasis shifted to capabilities (see Exhibit 2.7). Position is no longer enough in these newly defined competitive arenas.

Exhibit 2.5.   Alliances Result in Higher ROI

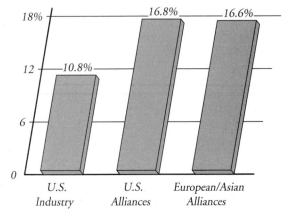

Average Return on Investment

Source: Authors' survey of 2,500 alliances, 1989–1993, and study of 120 non-U.S. alliances, 1994–1995.

Exhibit 2.6.   Alliance Drivers Evolve: Companies Race Toward Global Capabilities

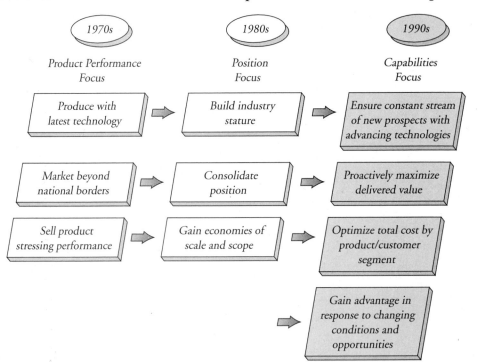

Exhibit 2.7. Position Is Perishable: Building and Renewing Capabilities Is Key

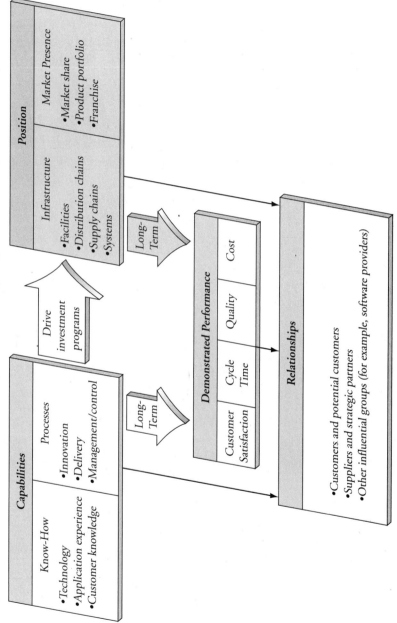

The name of the game is to maximize delivered value, to minimize total cost, and thereby to gain advantage.

Consider how these forces play out in various industries. The computer, telecommunications, and electronics industries (the upper-right quadrant of Exhibit 2.8) are excellent examples of how technology advances have created the need to build or quickly access new capabilities that were not previously relevant. To remain competitive, these industries also need to establish a global reach. In search of these goals, AT&T has formed more than four hundred alliances since 1990. BellSouth, which began as a regional telephone company in the southeastern United States, recently allied with Safra Group, a banking concern, and two other partners to provide cellular telephone service in São Paulo,

Exhibit 2.8.   Alliances Are Driven by Globalization Needs and Capability Gaps

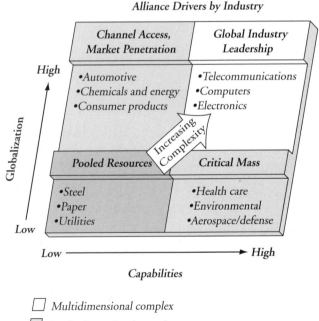

Source: Booz·Allen & Hamilton analysis.

Brazil. "We view this as the crown jewel of our Latin American strategy," said Duane Ackerman, BellSouth's chairman and CEO, quoted in the July 10, 1997, *Wall Street Journal.* "The size and magnitude of the market and the potential growth rate are very meaningful to us." For industries seeking to grow both capabilities and global reach, the biggest challenges are in the area of *partner assessment,* which includes screening partners, assessing risk, and identifying cross-cultural and implementation issues.

In other industries, such as those with health care or environmental companies, globalization has been less important than building a critical mass of capabilities (see the lower-right quadrant of Exhibit 2.8). Over time, however, globalization is becoming an important issue for these industries as well. The biggest issues here are in the area of *risk assessment.* Companies in these industries need to decide whether to seek an alliance, to seek an acquisition, or to develop the needed capability internally. A particular challenge is the assessment of the capability the potential partner brings, given that the partner is often involved in another industry. When Microsoft, which dominates computing through its software, and General Electric, which owns the NBC television network as well as local stations and cable operations, agreed to an alliance, they went through this process carefully.

In contrast, in the automotive, airline, chemicals, energy, and consumer products industries, the corporate objectives are to gain access to new regions rather than to seek capabilities. New capabilities are less important because industry lines are not blurring. Reflecting this, many alliances in these industries have been between competitors. For industries in this quadrant (the upper-left on Exhibit 2.8), the biggest issues are cross-cultural differences and partner assessment. PepsiCo, for instance, formed a very successful alliance with Lipton, the tea company owned by Unilever. The two drink makers were able to leverage each other's strengths, and the great increase in distribution of Lipton's iced tea produced a surge in market share. One victim was Quaker Oats, which had paid $1.7 billion for the Snapple beverage company but could not compete effectively with the Pepsi-Lipton alliance. After a change in management, Quaker Oats wound up shedding Snapple and taking a billion-dollar bath.

The Gap Between the Experienced and the Inexperienced

One key finding of all our surveys on alliances is clear: financial results improve dramatically as a company gains alliance experience. Indeed, companies experienced in alliances earn twice the return on investment in their alliances as do inexperienced companies (see Exhibit 2.9). This improvement in ROI is no statistical fluke. Although the degree of improvement varies widely from one industry to another, improvement shows up in almost every industry. And in some—consumer products, manufacturing, and telecommunications—the results are particularly dramatic, with fourfold and fivefold increases as experience takes hold. In simple terms, the "I" in the ROI is lower and the "R" is higher: companies active in alliances realize more bang for the buck (or the yen or the pound, for that matter). Unsurprisingly, as ROI soars, executives report a greater degree of satisfaction.

The benefits of alliance experience are pronounced in many European and Asian companies, which are generally more experienced in alliances than are their counterparts in the United States. There are historical, cultural, geographic, and regulatory explanations for European and Asian companies' greater strategic alliance activity, and these

Exhibit 2.9.   ROI Grows as Alliance Experience Increases

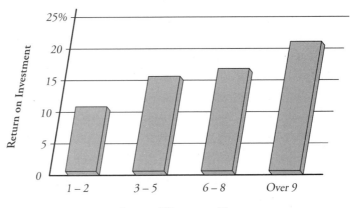

Source: Authors' survey of 2,500 alliances, 1989–1993.

are explored at length in Chapter Six. But in the 1960s, the creation of European and Asian strategic alliances accelerated rapidly, in response to the view that the United States was an economic colossus that threatened other nations' home markets. This perception was eloquently detailed in Jean-Jacques Servan-Schreiber's *The American Challenge,* published in 1967. The Europeans and Japanese did not have the scale of production or the resources to fight off a direct assault from the United States, Servan-Schreiber asserted: only through broader and deeper alliances could the American challenge be blunted.

By the early 1980s, their alliances enabled European and Japanese companies to mount a challenge in the home markets of U.S. industries. Strong U.S. industries, such as the shipbuilding, auto, photocopier, steel, and aerospace industries, faced vigorous competition, and they were often unprepared for it. From 1980 to 1990, companies based in the nations of the European Community (now the European Union) formed more than nine times as many alliances as companies in the United States. In addition, far more alliances in Europe and Asia involved equity stakes.

Over time, many U.S. companies have come to feel they need to form alliances to respond to these challenges. But the Europeans and Japanese continue to reap the benefits of their greater experience and longer-term relationships. And this experience factor is becoming even more important as the number of alliances forged across borders grows. The majority of alliances formed today involve cross-border transactions (see Exhibit 1.3); outside the United States nearly all alliances cross national borders.

However, in the early stages of alliance formation—the identification and evaluation of potential partners and the initial complex negotiation—perceptions of potential partners' abilities play a telling role, and our research shows that European and Asian companies avoid U.S. companies that are inexperienced in alliances. European executives, for example, find that many U.S. executives need to attend more to the processes that follow the negotiations, the critical alliance skills of planning integration and implementing. However, the Europeans do give Americans high grades for their skills in screening for partners and in assessing leverage, impact on stakeholders, and bargaining power.

As U.S. companies look abroad for partners, in addition to recognizing the greater Asian and European experience and perception of

U.S. executives' experience, they need to recognize that the stakes required to participate are growing. The average global strategic alliance investment by the top one thousand companies in the United States is $40 million. Asian companies, in contrast, invest an average of $90 million and European countries $150 million. Thus U.S. alliances also report lower sales per alliance: an average of $80 million compared with the alliance average of more than $250 million in Europe, where alliances are older as well as having more invested in them.

For years, strategic alliances and cooperative strategies were simply not part of the way most U.S. companies did business, especially in domestic markets. But as individual companies read their internal signs of declining investment in new businesses, a slowing of technical innovation, and a comparative weakening of business skills, alliances have become more attractive, as we discussed in Chapter One, bringing new capabilities to companies. The tidal wave of mergers and acquisitions of the 1980s and the subsequent downsizings of the 1990s make up yet another reason for the difficulties many companies in the United States are encountering in delivering adequate value to customers and replenishing their base of skills.

Moreover, the U.S. share of world exports had dropped up to 1995, whereas the shares of Japan, Germany, South Korea, Singapore, and Hong Kong have grown. The fifty largest non-U.S. companies are growing more quickly than the fifty largest U.S. companies (Boeing and General Electric being two notable exceptions). The external debt of the United States continues to grow more quickly than that of Japan or Germany, and this places pressure on companies and the U.S. government to raise capital. The pressure is increased by the continuing escalation of technology development costs in health care, electronics, computers, and telecommunications.

These pressures to compete, statistics on the general economy and on the financial benefits of alliances, and changing corporate drivers explain precisely why U.S. chief executives have come to view alliances more positively in recent years, moving from 20 percent in 1990 to nearly 60 percent in 1995. The comparable figures for European and Asian CEOs are 60 percent and 70 percent (see Exhibit 0.1). In their thinking about alliances, U.S. CEOs have dramatically closed the gap with European and Asian CEOs.

A survey of CEOs conducted by the Conference Board in 1994 provides similar evidence. CEOs in the United States, Mexico, and Europe were asked to rate how important strategic alliances were to their firms' core businesses. Eighty-one percent of the Mexican, 70 percent of the U.S., and 68 percent of the European CEOs said such alliances were "important" or "very important." Asked about their various goals in pursuing strategic alliances, Europeans said that increasing or maintaining market share was most important—cited by 90 percent, compared with 82 percent in Mexico and 74 percent in the United States. Geographic expansion was most important to 80 percent of U.S. executives. For the Mexican executives, technology or experience sharing was the top priority, with 87 percent (see Exhibit 2.10).

Exhibit 2.10.   CEO Alliance Goals Vary Little by Region

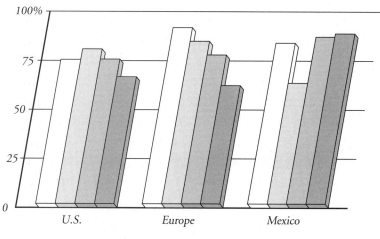

CEOs Rating Goal "Important"

Goals
☐ *Protect home market*
▨ *Geographic expansion*
▨ *Capability access*
■ *Technology sharing*

Source: Change Management: Strategic Alliances (a research report), The Conference Board, 1994.

Questions for Your Company

Now that many managers who previously chose to go it alone are seeking strategic alliances in record numbers, all managers must question the adequacy of the way they do business today. If they do not heed warning flags and do not consider strategic alliances as possible responses to their problems, they may wind up facing a consortium of competitors while having no alliance experience themselves. Every executive needs to consider whether strategic alliances are a path to continued growth. Completing the test in Exhibit 2.11 is a first step in assessing your company's alliance readiness.

If your total score on this test is 25 or less, alliances do not appear to be a critical priority for your company. A score of 26 to 55 indicates that your company should indeed give some thought to strategic alliances, perhaps using as a base some transactional alliances it has already formed. If your total is 56 or more, strategic alliances should be a high priority. Whatever your score, you must assess not only your company's attitude toward alliances but also how that attitude compares with the attitudes of other players in your industry.

How, then, to proceed? Executives, particularly those with limited experience in alliance formation, will want to find ways to leapfrog the learning curve and avoid the pain so often experienced by beginners. Such shortcuts require a disciplined approach and an understanding of the best practices that successful alliances builders use, as we illustrate in the following chapters.

Exhibit 2.11.   Test Your Company's Alliance Needs

Rate your company in each category, using the following scale:

Not a factor	Very little	Little impact	Moderate	Somewhat high	High	Very high
1	2	3	4	5	6	7

Key Strategic Issues/Degrees of Pressure	Rating
Technology base. Your industry is experiencing a rapidly escalating technology base	_____
Overseas access. You are frustrated with the difficulty of penetrating a foreign market where the opportunity is attractive	_____
Related-market segment access. You are dissatisfied with leveraging your strength with a new growth opportunity	_____
Gaining economies. Your company is not adopting new productivity methods as quickly as you would like	_____
Risk sharing. An increasing research-and-development burden is being felt by your company and your industry	_____
Management skills. Your edge in core competencies is under pressure by capable competitors	_____
Funding constraints. You are faced with increasingly heavy investment burdens, and you want to leverage scarce resources	_____
Changing distribution channels. Destabilizing conditions are forcing a new look at delivery alternatives in your markets	_____
Value-added barriers to competition. You want to strengthen value-added skills and raise the level of competitive intensity within your industry	_____
Barriers to acquisition. Opportunities are limited because of size, geography, or ownership reluctance at loss of control	_____
TOTAL SCORE	_____

Chapter 3
Leapfrogging the Learning Curve

The more alliances you do, the better you get at them. So how can newcomers make up for lost time? After more than a decade of surveying companies around the world and interviewing hundreds of their top executives, we have developed an alliance methodology with four stages:

1. Identification
2. Valuation
3. Negotiation
4. Implementation

These four stages encompass eight activities, or steps: defining strategy and objectives, screening for partners, assessing tradeables and leverage, defining opportunity, assessing the impact on stakeholders, assessing bargaining power, planning integration, and implementing.

One error that less-experienced companies all too frequently make is to jump into the process at the point of opportunity definition. This failure to couple alliance formation with strategic thinking and the consequent failure to lay down a strong foundation almost without exception create disabling problems.

Recently, for example, we were invited to a major pharmaceutical firm to discuss alliance building. As we walked down a corridor, one division president asked us to step into his office, then closed the door. "I have eighteen exciting alliance proposals on my desk," he said. "Would you look at them and give me an opinion before you leave? There's a lot of pressure here to make something happen!" We were reminded of Alice's encounter with the Cheshire Cat, when she asked which way she should go:

> "That depends a good deal on where you want to get to," said the Cat.
> "I don't much care where—" said Alice.
> "Then it doesn't matter which way you go," said the Cat.

Examining alliance opportunities without defining alliance strategy and objectives is quite similar; it's not going to matter which one you choose.

There are plenty of other common traps, also known as painful learning experiences, for companies trying to form alliances. Fortunately, there are also underlying principles and best practices to help executives avoid the traps and be successful faster. Because the pitfalls, principles, and practices apply across the stages and activities of alliance building, we present them here as part of a foundation for learning about the methodology. Chapter Four continues to build that foundation with case studies, and we discuss the methodology itself in Chapter Five.

Key Principles

Our experience and our observations of many successful and failed negotiations and alliances show that as the most experienced and best-managed companies contemplate strategic alliances, they are guided by several key principles:

- *Go strength to strength.* Alliances should always be formed on a strength-to-strength basis. A company that tries to improve its weak position by securing a strong partner most often finds itself dominated by the stronger partner. An alliance with one weak player allied to another weak player is not likely to pose much of a challenge to stronger rivals.

• *Focus on incremental value.* Concentrate on making the pie bigger rather than worrying about your slice. Instead of emphasizing learning a partner's skills, emphasize building skills incremental to the combined entity. Also avoid getting bogged down in how ownership will be shared until you and your partner have fully agreed on the nature and quantification of incremental value.

• *Gradually build relationships.* Step-by-step, build consensus and trust immediately from the start. Avoid loose and ragged partnership agreements. Start with something concrete and manageable, and then expand the relationship's scope.

• Be *structurally adaptable.* No one way to organize the alliance is right. A 50–50 or 33–33–33 arrangement does offer the advantage of equal footing, but it can also lead to an inefficient allocation of workload. The focus should not be ownership share but advantaged capability. In the Airbus consortium, for example, attempts to spread production evenly across the four partners led to the building of redundant capability in several countries rather than making best use of each partner's strengths and rationalizing capability. Yes, a 50–50 relationship does offer legal safeguards to both partners—but the best alliances are built on cooperation, not legal safeguards. One of our U.S. clients takes a more sophisticated approach and lets equity shares be unbalanced, but requires equal representation on the alliance's board. A Japanese client focuses its attention on getting control of key management appointments, letting its U.S. partners have the illusion of control through majority ownership.

Alliance Best Practices: Key Success Factors

Beyond these broad principles is the glue that holds alliances together. That glue is best practices, which enable companies to move smoothly from one stage of alliance building to the next.

Over years of surveys—identifying more than six thousand alliances involving over five hundred companies—and hundreds of interviews, and comparisons of more and less experienced and successful alliance builders, we were able to identify one hundred best practices that contribute to the success of a strategic alliance (we describe our methods in more detail in Chapter Five). Through further comparison, we then determined the following seven best practices that are most closely linked to superior results. (Exhibits 3.1 through 3.7 compare the capabilities of experienced and less-experienced companies for carrying out each of the best practices. The survey on which the exhibits are based examined 283 companies having nearly two thousand alliances and involved nearly one hundred interviews.)

Best Practice 1: Preparing a Realistic Feasibility Study

Managers experienced in alliance building emphasize the assumptions, rigor, analytical depth, and consistency of an alliance business plan much more than do those who are inexperienced (see Exhibit 3.1). Alliance veterans often seek the help of outside experts, especially when an alliance will bring them into unfamiliar markets. This early assessment can then be directly translated into an explicit operating plan and budget.

The experienced firms have learned that direction setting is more complicated in alliances than in individual companies because of the difficulties of establishing and maintaining harmonious communica-

Exhibit 3.1. Capability for Preparing a Realistic Feasibility Study

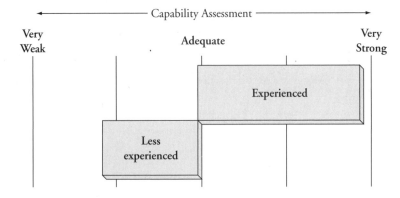

Source: Authors' survey of 283 companies.

tion between the partners. An alliance plan may be analytically sound, but its chances of success also depend on many indeterminate elements. The competitive reactions to the alliance, corporate culture, organizational structure, resource base, overall fit with a partner's long-term strategy, and willingness of partners to commit high-caliber people and resources to the alliance all play major roles in an alliance's progress.

To avoid raising hurdles in these areas, a process for building broad consensus among internal and external stakeholders is needed. Experienced companies not only prepare good alliance plans but also calculate a probability of success after examining the effects of all the variables on the alliance. Failing to factor in even one variable can produce disastrous results, as International Business Machines learned when it focused on personal computers. IBM executives calculated that the fastest way to create a market for personal computers was to ally the firm's huge base of technological expertise with the MS-DOS operating system provided by Microsoft and the microprocessors created by Intel. In the very short run, IBM was successful, but it failed to factor in competitive reaction. Because IBM was relying on software and hardware that were not proprietary, it could not control the market. Hundreds of smaller, more nimble competitors—the *clone makers*—were able to use the same Microsoft and Intel technology to create competitive machines, often with more features and lower prices. IBM lost its dominant position in personal computing to Compaq Computer, Dell Computer, and others and has never regained it.

Best Practice 2: Anticipating Business Risks and Mitigating Them

Experienced managers concentrate on understanding the key risks that an alliance poses and considering how to deal with them (see Exhibit 3.2). Among the critical issues that come up often are these:

- Predicting the effect the alliance will have on the long-term competitiveness of the parent companies—*beware of creating a new competitor!*
- Anticipating resistance to and resentment of change—*How will the organization react?*

Exhibit 3.2.   Capability for Anticipating and Mitigating Key Business Risks

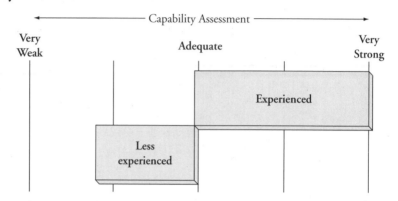

Source: Authors' survey of 283 companies.

- Doing a short-and long-term trade-off analysis—*What does the alliance mean to the company over the long haul?*
- Foreseeing the interchange of proprietary information and processes—*Are we giving up too much?*
- Preparing for a possible breakdown of communications—*What level of trust do we need and expect?*
- Tailoring management systems and processes to the alliance's unique requirements—*What organizational structure does the alliance need, and can we live with it?*

Plans by inexperienced managers typically do not identify such risks and thus invite undesirable consequences later on. Consider the problems encountered by the Brooke Group after it formed a strategic alliance in 1991 with Ducat, one of the largest cigarette makers in the former Soviet Union. With Mikhail Gorbachev's encouragement and support, an alliance was created, hoping to capitalize on a cigarette shortage so grave that protests erupted against the government. From a business point of view, demand was enormous; from a political point of view, the alliance could alleviate unrest. But with the end of the Communist government, the official government agencies with which the alliance had been negotiated ceased to exist. Then an audit found that the Ducat factory was loaded with debt, supplies were missing, and hard currency from the company's treasury had been embezzled. When Brooke's management moved to fire the Ducat factory director, he hired former KGB officers as security guards. With no clear due process of law in the unsettled environment, Brooke had little choice but to negotiate a severance package with the accused manager. Despite the enormous business opportunity, the alliance never brought a single cigarette to market.

In hindsight it was clear that Brooke, like many companies new to alliance building, had paid much more attention to the opportunity than it had to potential problems. Brooke failed to ask what might happen to the enterprise if the government that encouraged and supported it were changed.

Best Practice 3: Linking Budgets to Resources and Priorities

Experienced alliance builders feel strongly that a key to success is linking budgets to resources and strategic priorities (see Exhibit 3.3). Our survey results clearly show that experienced companies focus more on priority development and resource development than on short-term results. They also devote considerable effort to finding high-caliber personnel and to

Exhibit 3.3.   Capability for Linking Budgets to Resources and Priorities

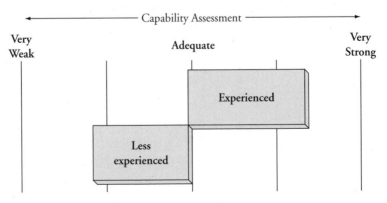

Source: Authors' survey of 283 companies.

carefully matching individuals to strategic priorities and objectives. In contrast, inexperienced companies often try to build alliances on the cheap, skipping steps in the alliance-building framework.

Best Practice 4: Conducting Realistic Partner Assessment and Selection

Partner selection is of critical importance in any alliance. Inexperienced firms often fail to pay enough attention to this, concentrating on their objectives and rationales instead of conducting a detailed analysis of potential partners (see Exhibit 3.4). Too often they approach an alliance as if it were an acquisition, concentrating much effort on details of price and legal steps and too little on what will happen next.

We recently lunched with the senior executive of a Fortune 100 corporation who said his various companies had already formed more than fifty strategic alliances. Yet governance problems were surfacing in many of them, he said, and issues kept emerging that had not been anticipated beforehand. "What a headache!" he complained. His attitude was that the alliances themselves were the problem, rather than the way they had been approached.

Exhibit 3.4.   Capability for Conducting Realistic Partner Assessment and Selection

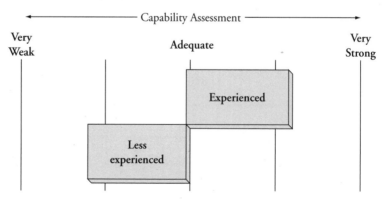

Source: Authors' survey of 283 companies.

In contrast, successful alliance builders have knowledge of the potential partner's management culture, its previous alliance experience, and its strategic objectives. They try to acknowledge these perspectives and make allowances to accommodate them in the negotiations leading up to a deal. The best managers understand a potential partner's core strengths and weaknesses, and they understand the differences between a horizontal (same industry) and a vertical (different industry) fit. No matter what the time pressure, they avoid rushing into situations where their own preparation is not complete. "We do our homework to determine if our potential partners know the process," one manager at a Fortune 500 company told us. And significantly, these experienced alliance builders also consider and negotiate divorce procedures, penalties for poor performance, and methods of arbitration.

Best Practice 5: Adopting Superior Resource Strategy Planning

Experienced companies recognize that alliances require superior resource planning to generate the added value that a collaboration promises (see Exhibit 3.5). And superior planning is more effective when partners demonstrate their commitment to the alliance by clearly specifying the

Exhibit 3.5. Capability for Adopting Superior Resource Strategy Planning

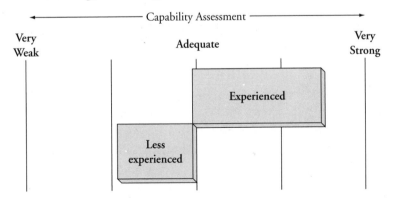

Source: Authors' survey of 283 companies.

quality and level of resources that each will allocate. Without this effort, amicable relationships can dissolve quickly. Experienced companies openly discuss each partner's contribution of people, money, and other resources. They prepare precise timetables of when and how resources will be available, secured, transferred, and delivered. They make certain that the resources devoted to the alliance are of the highest caliber. Inexperienced companies might do well to employ a facilitator during this planning, to help partners establish the communication and trust that will serve as a solid foundation for their alliance.

Cytel's success in alliances exemplifies the benefits of superior resource planning. In 1991, Cytel, a small biotechnology firm in the United States, negotiated a technology development agreement with Sumitomo Pharmaceuticals of Japan to develop drugs based on Cytel's technology. Both sides were clear about what the alliance would produce and what benefits would accrue to each partner: in exchange for the option to license products for Pacific Rim markets, Sumitomo agreed to provide $15 million for research and development over a five-year period. If products emerged, Sumitomo had the right to market them, paying a fee as well as royalties on sales. The agreement also required Sumitomo to make an equity investment of $5 million in Cytel. Both parties clearly understood that products for the commercial market might not emerge for years, and they were content with this. Many partners might not have had the patience for such a strategy.

Best Practice 6: Coupling Investment and Rewards with Performance.

Experienced alliance managers avoid open-ended investment postures (see Exhibit 3.6). Being clear with stakeholders—be they unions, banks, suppliers, customers—about alliance objectives helps bring to the surface early on any problems that might otherwise make themselves known only much later. How will these different parties see the alliance? Problems and questions they raise need to be addressed before your company enters the starting gate. Experienced companies create performance measures and link them to pay and investment. Compensation packages need to be flexible and entrepreneurial to reflect the nature of the project.

Exhibit 3.6.   Capability for Coupling Investment and Rewards with Performance

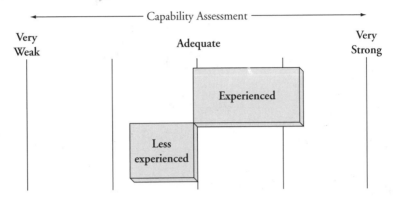

Source: Authors' survey of 283 companies.

People's worries that working for an alliance could derail their company careers must be addressed, and resolving these concerns often requires different incentives than those appropriate at the parent company.

"Do you know what the difference is between you and us when it comes to alliance building?" a prominent European executive once said to us. "When we send the alliance boat out from the mother ship, we provide life preservers. When you send the alliance boat out, you don't—and you will not listen to the screams if it sinks."

No one should forget the risks taken by the operating manager and by the employees who are asked to make an alliance work. Companies need creative ways to provide a sense of security and motivation for these people. Appropriate life preservers include balloon payments, severance packages, lifelines back to the parent ship, and phantom stock programs. Absent such considerations, alliance employees frequently become disgruntled. They also need compensation rewards aligned with strategic performance.

Best Practice 7: Clearly Defining Managers' Roles

Although successful companies avoid the typical decision-making-by-committee process, they do specify the responsibilities and authority of alliance managers and adopt a periodic structured review process (see Exhibit 3.7). They also plan to build strong working and reporting

Exhibit 3.7.   Capability for Clearly Defining Managers' Roles

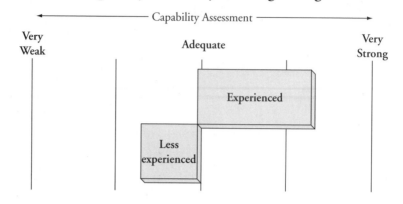

Source: Authors' survey of 283 companies.

relationships, both external and internal, and to foster loyalty to the alliance rather than the parents. That is precisely what British Petroleum and Mobil did in their European alliance (as we explore in Chapter Four).

Pitfalls to Avoid

For many companies and executives, the experience of trying to forge a strategic alliance is comparable to adolescence: they suffer from inexperience, they have a hard time learning from the mistakes of others, and too often they insist on going it alone. Searching through the rubble of failed and failing alliances, we have identified seven traps to avoid.

1. *Being a possessive child* (focusing on one's own slice of the pie and who controls the baker, rather than trying to grow the pie). The key to overcoming possessive child syndrome is to switch emphasis from control to value creation. Too many alliance partners seem more concerned with who owns what share than with how much incremental value can be created through the coupling of their capabilities. All partners must keep in mind that mutual benefit is a critical element for a successful alliance.

Some companies are staking their futures on consortiums. For example, seeking a standard for a new CD technology that will store feature-length films on a single disk (known as DVD, for digital video disk), Time Warner helped form a consortium that includes Sony, Philips, Hitachi, Matsushita, Mitsubishi, Victor Co. of Japan, Pioneer Electronics, Toshiba, and Thomson Multimedia. In another consortium that is staking out a major claim in the market for satellite broadcasting services, Time Warner has joined with Bell Atlantic, Ameritech, and Tele-Communications Inc.

2. *Seeing through the eyes of a juvenile* (failing to develop the right amount of trust). Some alliances fail because of a lack of trust. At one extreme, alliances are negotiated with extremely detailed, overly rigorous legal documents. Then, as they begins their work, issues often arise that require lengthy discussions among corporate lawyers. Executives wind up being drawn into these discussions, and stagnation follows. At the other extreme, alliances founder because partners enter into arrangements too quickly. Trusting only vague agreements, believing that arrangements can be adjusted as needed on the fly no matter what the state of the alliance at that time, is a formula for failure.

A far better course is to develop an alliance that is based both on trust and on each party's articulation of its own objectives and acknowledgment of the other's objectives. Often the best people to handle these arrangements are line managers. These are the people who will have to get the job done, and if they are uncomfortable with some aspects of the proposed alliances, the chances of its succeeding diminish. We suggest that the middle-line management be involved early in the alliance negotiations. Only when these managers are satisfied should corporate lawyers and corporate staff join the negotiations.

When Dow Corning was formed by Dow Chemical and Corning fifty-five years ago, the two CEOs formed the alliance on a handshake. Nine months later, after the venture was already up and running, the lawyers completed the paperwork.

3. *Causing a generation gap* (depending on inadequate or erratic communications). Sometimes cooperation fever grows so swiftly that it threatens to sweep away good sense. Starting an alliance without a clear

understanding of all parties' cultural dynamics and organizational resistance to change is like playing Russian roulette. Without clear, open, and regular communication, an unbridgeable gap can open, with the parties talking past each other as tension, frustration, and suspicion grow.

The source of such communication problems is often a bureaucracy bound up in the traditional ways of doing business. Like their counterparts in Russia as that nation emerged from the Communist years, corporate apparatchiks are unfamiliar and uncomfortable with fostering partnership and working at a faster and more flexible pace. Like some elected officials, corporate leaders often assume that once an order is given, the bureaucracy will fall into line. But as former president Gerald Ford once said of the U.S. presidency, "The most frustrating part of the job is knowing full well that many commands the Presidents give will just never be carried out." An antidote to bureaucratic gridlock is frequent and regular communication, ensuring that attitudes are monitored and that enthusiasm, support, and trust are forthcoming.

4.   *Dodging the draft* (failing to attract the best individuals to the alliance). One common symptom in an ailing alliance is that employees confide, "I'm out of the company's mainstream, and my career has stopped dead." Successful alliances require personal commitments, yet they are inherently high risk from a career perspective. If the alliance fails, the individuals who worked on it may find themselves stuck on a ship drifting or barely afloat while the mother ship charts a new course. It is essential to a successful alliance that it draw on its partners' best employees and not become a dumping ground for misfits. The alliance must also draw on the entrepreneurial spirit of top managers and not become a parking space for executives awaiting retirement. The solution is for the partners to make clear that alliance participation is a career enhancer. A company must build a track record of rescuing its people and returning them with honor should an alliance turn sour.

One alliance that successfully tapped the entrepreneurial spirit of its partners brought together Northwestern Mutual Life and Dun & Bradstreet. The alliance began inconspicuously enough: a senior D&B executive whose daughter was thinking of attending Vanderbilt University called an executive vice president at Northwestern Mutual who was an alumnus of the school. After a chat about campus life, the conversation turned to business matters of mutual interest and eventually led to an alliance for a marketing information system to help Northwestern Mutual insurance agents penetrate the small to medium-sized business sector. Dun & Bradstreet took the lead in developing the business information system and on-line support, and Northwestern Mutual supported the development program, trained the agents, developed insurance products for the new market, and created test sites within its own organization. Because of the strong relationship that developed between the two executives who first made contact, the best people were identified in each company, from computer and telemarketing specialists to million-dollar-club insurance agents. Each company went out of its way to ensure high-quality resources; each company assured its employees that no one's career would suffer for participating in the alliance. So successful was the alliance that D&B used it as a model for more than fifty others worldwide.

5. *Picking the wrong spouse* (failing to take the time to select the right partner). In business, as in life, picking the wrong spouse inevitably leads to disastrous consequences. Yet too many alliances begin with one company reacting to overtures from another company rather than undertaking an active, vigorous, and thoughtful assessment of its own capability gaps and a prioritization of its ideal partners. Getting to know a potential partner's culture and how it influences behavior inside and outside the partner company is an important aspect of alliance building. It is also important to acknowledge that selection of one partner may foreclose other partner options, even in unrelated areas. One multi-segment company forged a promising relationship with a South Korean chaebol (a large, family-controlled conglomerate), only to find that the other chaebols subsequently refused to discuss more optimal alliances with its other operating units.

6. *Being vague about the prenuptials* (failing to agree explicitly on objectives and goals). Whatever agreements are finally worked out between alliance partners, the provisions provide an early glimpse of how the relationship will develop over time. An explicit understanding of each other's objectives and expectations, gives partners the opportunity to

maximize overall value and reduce misunderstandings that will surface along the way. Conversely, entering negotiations without conducting a thorough tradeables and leverage analysis of one's own strengths and weaknesses can lead to a miscalculation of one's bargaining position.

At the other end of the relationship—measuring an alliance's success—clarity and understanding of the partners' goals is just as important. Success can be measured in improvement in return on investment, market share, product quality, technical knowledge, and costs. To avoid the uneasy situation where one partner is trumpeting the alliance's success while the other is far less happy, an agreement on measures is essential. A number of companies have rated alliances as unsatisfactory, whatever the return on investment, because company strategic goals were unmet. Lucky Goldstar of South Korea, for example, was unhappy with the results of several alliances with Japanese companies because the Japanese would not provide access to technology that Lucky Goldstar had assumed it could gain from its partners.

7. *Living with the in-laws* (solving the protective parent syndrome). Well-meaning parents can be stifling when they impose their own culture and philosophy on their children, and the same is true in corporate life. Managers of an alliance face different challenges than parent companies' managers do and usually require different processes, structures, and cultures to address the alliance's environment successfully. The emerging organization must be shaped to reflect the unique needs of the alliance. The classic alliance between Standard Oil of California, or Socal (now Chevron), and Texaco forged in 1936 remains one of the best examples of how parents can avoid overly protecting their offspring.

Socal had the oil concession in Bahrain but did not have access to refineries that could handle the high-sulfur oil it pumped there. Texaco had extensive marketing operations in Africa and Asia but had no supply of Middle East oil. So they agreed on an alliance, Caltex, that pulled together each company's assets "east of Suez," and they put in place managers with the authority to handle those assets as the managers saw fit (see Exhibit 3.8). At its peak, Caltex produced more than 1.1 million barrels of crude oil a day, and it now markets its products in more

Exhibit 3.8.   Caltex: A Case Study

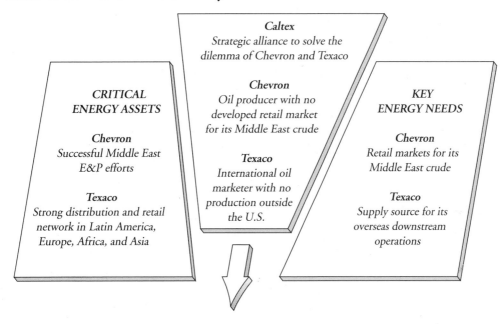

Source: Booz·Allen & Hamilton analysis.

than fifty countries, producing revenue of more than $11 billion. It remains one of the most attractive assets of Chevron and Texaco.

The Additional Factor of Organizational Complexity

Part of avoiding pitfalls on the one hand and employing best practices on the other is understanding that not all best practices have equal relevance in every strategic alliance. The approach needs to be tailored to each situation.

Experienced executives have learned to take note of what we call a *complexity boundary.* We find it necessary to tailor a business's approach to strategic alliances to that business's nature and capabilities—what we think of as its organizational complexity. This complexity is defined by the level of research and development a company uses, the variety and number of its products or services, its international scope, and the extent to which new products contribute to its revenue and growth. We have found that *mixed alliances,* those between complex and simple companies, generally fail precisely because the best practices that work for each type of company are different. Less-complex companies, for example, pay more attention to operational matters and timetables and less to communications and lines of authority. To better understand how strong alliances are forged, in the next chapter we look at a few notable alliances and the lessons they offer.

Chapter 4
How Great Alliances Grew
Four Case Studies

Four case studies of highly successful alliances illustrate in action not only the four stages of alliance building—identification, valuation, negotiation, and implementation—but also the key principles we emphasized earlier, particularly the importance of joining strength to strength. And they reveal how alliances produce not only expected but often considerable unexpected benefits and how even competitors can achieve their different goals through a common endeavor.

Fuji Photo Film and Xerox

The alliance of Xerox and Fuji Photo Film stands as one of the most successful partnerships of the last three decades, a striking example of how planning, negotiation (both before and after the agreement was struck), and adaptability have provided a powerful engine for profitability and innovation.

It started modestly enough: in 1962, the parent companies created Fuji Xerox, a 50–50 joint venture, whose intended mission was to market Xerox's copying products in Japan and to use that base in order to market to Indonesia, the Philippines, South Korea, Taiwan, and the countries of Indochina. Xerox placed its 50 percent in the hands of

Rank Xerox, an earlier alliance between Xerox and the Rank Organization of Britain.

In seeking out and negotiating the alliance with Fuji, Xerox primarily sought entry into the Asian market through a local partner. Fuji's goal in accepting the alliance was to diversify from the traditional photo film business, where it was and remains the number two worldwide producer, behind Eastman Kodak. Each company saw the alliance primarily as a way to market copiers.

But then the project was altered, almost from the start. The Japanese government would not grant approval to the joint venture if Fuji Xerox was to be no more than a marketing company, so Xerox and Fuji revised their plan. Fuji Xerox was invested with manufacturing rights in addition to its marketing responsibilities, and eventually with manufacturing capability as well. (Initially, the manufacturing was carried out in Fuji Photo plants; in 1970, those plants were transferred to Fuji Xerox.) This component of the alliance, added solely to obtain government approval, became a growth engine that later came to the rescue of Xerox.

In the alliance's early days, Xerox's plain-paper copiers were dominating the marketplace to an extraordinary degree, with a market share of more than 90 percent. Indeed, the corporate name became—and remains—a synonym for photocopy. Xerox's growth was phenomenal, with revenues vaulting to $1.2 billion in 1966 from a mere $40 million six years earlier.

But by the 1970s, Xerox was in jeopardy. It had focused on high-powered rivals like Eastman Kodak and IBM, which were threatening its lucrative mid-and high-end markets; now Japanese competitors were assaulting the low end. Pressured by U.S. antitrust regulators, in 1975 Xerox was forced to agree to make many of its patents available with small or no licensing fees. (In another blow, Xerox was forced to allow outside companies to service the copiers it leased to its customers.) Between the Xerox technologies and those they developed on their own, the Japanese rivals made deep inroads and ate more than a third of Xerox's market share.

"The Japanese were selling products in the United States for what it cost us to make them," said David Kearns, Xerox's chief executive at the time, as Benjamin Gomes-Casseres recounts in "Competing in Constellations: The Case of Fuji Xerox" (*Strategy & Business,* First Quarter, 1997). "We didn't have the cost structure to do anything about it." But to the astonishment and delight of Xerox's managers, Fuji Xerox came to the rescue.

From the very start of the alliance, many of the Japanese engineers at Fuji Xerox were trying, out of pride and self-interest, to develop technology that would make them less dependent on the parent companies. The initial efforts attempted to adapt Xerox designs to the Japanese market, which generally wanted smaller machines than the mainline Xerox models and which used different standard paper sizes.

Next, as Gomes-Casseres also describes, Fuji Xerox managers took advantage of the unusual autonomy granted them by Xerox and Fuji Photo and decided to try to create a compact, inexpensive high-performance machine. By the end of the decade, they had prototypes, and in 1970, they demonstrated their work to Rank Xerox executives in London. The prototype was more compact than any copier Xerox had produced, and its manufacturing costs were projected at half those of the smallest Xerox machines.

The audacious alliance team made its name with that project, and for the first time Fuji Xerox received specific research and development funding from its parents. As the small copier became a best-seller, Fuji Xerox's engineering and manufacturing capabilities were acclaimed; in 1980, the company received the Japanese government's W. Edwards Deming prize for achieving outstanding quality. In the ensuing years, Fuji Xerox became hugely successful and a growth engine for both parents, in large part because Fuji and Xerox had staffed the alliance shrewdly and then stepped back and let the alliance managers do their jobs.

Led first by Setsutaro Kobayashi and later by his son, Yotaro Kobayashi (who succeeded his father as president in 1978), Fuji Xerox made enormous strides. Because it was based in Japan, the enterprise was well positioned to respond to the greatest threat to Xerox's dominance of the copier market—the innovations of Ricoh, Canon, and Minolta. "The fact that we had this strong company in Japan was of extraordinary importance when other Japanese companies started coming after us," Xerox chief executive Paul A. Allaire told Gomes-Casseres.

"Fuji Xerox was able to see them coming earlier and understood their development and manufacturing techniques."

In 1978, Rank Xerox began to purchase copiers made by Fuji Xerox to sell in Europe, and within a year Xerox had begun to do the same in the United States. The imports helped Xerox dampen the inroads made by Ricoh, Canon, and Minolta. Eventually Xerox managers came to see Fuji Xerox not just as a creator of low-cost machines but as a source of competitive information from the Japanese front. Technology *and* management techniques began to flow from Fuji Xerox back to Xerox.

Xerox managers were at first startled, for example, by how few component parts Fuji Xerox had to reject—which helped contain its manufacturing costs. Top executives and managers from Xerox and Rank Xerox began to visit Fuji Xerox to study its quality-control approach and other issues on the management agenda. Again learning from Fuji Xerox, Xerox trimmed the number of suppliers it relied on and, along the way, knocked down the cost of purchased parts by 45 percent. As Xerox learned and stabilized, so too did Fuji Xerox. By 1990, most of the copiers built and sold by Fuji Xerox were based on its own designs, and the vast majority of the low-end copiers sold by Xerox and Rank Xerox were provided by Fuji Xerox.

At the same time, Xerox and Fuji Xerox began to work together more closely. Strengthening communications, the top executives began to hold "summit meetings" twice a year. In addition, personnel exchange programs were put in place, then broadened. Joint research projects were used to avoid duplication of effort.

One goal of this closer collaboration was to compete with Canon in the business of computer printers. Canon dominated the market for printer engines, supplying them to the market leader, Hewlett-Packard as well as using them in its own printers. In 1991, Xerox and Fuji Xerox established Xerox International Partners, whose mission was to market Fuji Xerox printer engines outside of Japan. This new alliance also put Fuji Xerox into closer contact with U.S. customers.

The negotiations to set up this new alliance, which took more than a year, were revealing in their thoroughness. "A lot of bright people argued down all the alleys looking for potential future problems," Jefferson Kennard, Xerox director of Fuji Xerox relations, reported to Gomes-Casseres. "We spent our time going through all the 'what if' questions. We took the agreement apart and put it back together. Because of this searching, things should be pretty smooth. Throughout all these arguments, we maintained a long-term vision."

Note, particularly, the continuing adaptability of all the parties. Even though Fuji Xerox built its reputation and flourished by being largely autonomous, its management and its parents came to see that by the 1980s a closer collaboration was needed. To their credit, the managers of Fuji Photo, Xerox, and Fuji Xerox were able to respond to new challenges and new opportunities.

Corning and Siemens

Two leading industrial companies with strong reputations as technology innovators, Corning Inc. and Siemens AG, joined forces in 1973 to build and capitalize on the new and rapidly growing market for fiber-optic cable.

"After we developed the first practical optical fiber, we faced a marketing problem," recalled James Houghton, the chief executive of Corning, in a Booz·Allen & Hamilton interview. "Phone companies and other users do not buy fiber—they buy cable. We needed an enthusiastic cabler with no vested interest in the United States or in U.S. copper cable. Siemens had top-flight cable technology, so we formed two joint ventures with Siemens: one in Germany, which makes optical fiber, and one in the United States, which makes optical cable."

Creating Siecor, Siemens and Coming brought together their complementary capabilities in telecommunications and glass technology to build an independent joint venture that has gained a leadership position in the fiber-optic cable business. Corning had patented processes to manufacture high-quality optical fibers. Siemens had capital, scale, and worldwide distribution of telecommunications cable. Siemens also brought the manufacturing technology and equipment to turn the fiber into cable.

Each company was already experienced in alliances and could act with confidence; each held important patents for the project; each wanted to gain market access. The negotiations, though complex, were lubricated by the fact that the companies already had nonequity relationships involving sophisticated electronics equipment and some joint development projects. "There was a very foresighted guy at Siemens who said, 'Never mind this joint development agreement, let's form a 50–50 company and we'll call it Siecor,'" Richard Dulude, the retired vice chairman of Corning, recalled to C. K. Prahalad and Gary Hamel ("The Core Competence of the Corporation," *Harvard Business Review,* May–June 1990). "That was in 1973. For many years it was a development company, trying to make the fibers, make the cables and all the other kinds of devices that are necessary to make optical telecommunications a reality. And eventually we turned it into a manufacturing operation."

Siecor GmbH, created in 1973, is still operating. In 1977, Corning and Siemens formed Siecor Corporation, now one of the world's largest suppliers of optical cable. "We had found in the United States that the people who were in the telephone cable business, making copper cables, were not very enthused about fiber because they viewed it as a threat that was going to make them obsolete," Dulude said. "They weren't really working very diligently on it."

Siemens, the third-largest public company in Germany (after Daimler-Benz and Volkswagen) had been trying to find a door into the U.S. market. In the early 1970s, it acquired a few smaller telecommunications equipment companies in the United States, including Rolm. In Corning, Siemens teamed up with an esteemed and major player. Corning's many historic accomplishments included providing the glass for Thomas Edison's first lightbulb, in 1880. Siemens by then had already made its mark by building the 6,600-mile London-Calcutta telegraph link in 1870 and the first trans-Atlantic cable, connecting Ireland and the United States, in 1874.

Corning was also a patriarch of the strategic alliance business, sharing in some of the most successful and enduring alliances in business history. In 1937, it joined with Pittsburgh Plate Glass to form Pittsburgh Corning, which makes glass construction blocks; the following year, with Owens-Illinois, it formed Owens-Corning Fiberglass. In 1943, Corning and Dow Chemical created Dow Corning, to make silicones. More recent alliances have included Samsung-Corning, with the South Korean consumer electronics manufacturer, and Ciba-Corning, with Ciba-Geigy, the pharmaceutical giant.

Corning believes these alliances all profited from the equal standings of their parents. Robert Ecklin, a longtime senior vice president for industrial products at Corning, has said a 50–50 arrangement is both practical and symbolically important (Margaret Cauley de la Sierra, *Managing Global Alliances: Key Steps for Successful Collaboration,* 1995). "Most successful alliances are not managed or dictated by equity shareholdings," he observes. "Much of the success of a venture depends on the partners' ability to compromise on key issues. A 50–50 joint venture fosters such compromises and a give-and-take attitude. In essence, 50–50 joint ventures force the partners to try to get along."

Siemens, based in Munich, is also no stranger to alliances. Among its most important partnerships is one with its rivals in manufacturing computer chips, IBM and Toshiba, to develop the powerful chip known as the D-RAM, and another with Robert Bosch, also a German engineering giant, to create one of Europe's largest manufacturers of consumer appliances.

By 1978, it was clear to Corning and Siemens that the fiber-optic cable market was growing quickly. To rapidly expand their manufacturing capacity in the United States, Corning and Siemens acquired Superior Cable of North Carolina. "This was a $100 million cable company that had machinery we could use immediately," Houghton said. "They had access to the Baby Bells, as well as to some of the non-Bell telephone companies. In 1980, we merged Superior and Siecor. Today, we are the industry leader in optical fiber and cable and ancillary equipment."

In 1993, the base was broadened once again, through acquisition. Corning and Siecor paid $130 million to buy Northern Telecom's fiber-optic business. Siecor has also won a prominent role in Japan's fiber-optic cable market with its Siecor International unit.

"We overcame a problem in bringing our optical fiber to world markets," Houghton said. "In many parts of the world, telephone companies are still the principal customers of optical fiber. Although they are being privatized now, many are still monopolies owned and controlled by national governments. These institutions were unlikely to make a change from copper wire to optical fiber if the sole supplier was a U.S. firm, and that is understandable. No country wants to give up control of its telecommunications structure to a foreign firm. So we created 50–50 joint ventures in Germany, England, and Australia with firms that already had access to the local telephone systems."

The continuing success of Siecor comes as no surprise. "You can perhaps have only one goal," said Bernhard Plettner, president of Siemens when the Siecor alliance was created. "That is to be in the top group of most efficient firms" ("Siemens Secures Its Foothold in the U.S.," *Business Week,* Feb. 27, 1978).

At Corning, Van Campbell, the vice chairman, struck a similar note, as Stratford Sherman reported ("Are Strategic Alliances Working?" *Fortune,* Sept. 21, 1992): "We're looking only for lifetime associations. Because you have to invest an enormous amount of energy to make a partnership work. You not only have to deal with the business, you also constantly have to deal with the relationship you have with the partner—nurturing it and maintaining high-level contacts, so that when you deal with items of substance you will be dealing with friends, people you understand and respect."

Wal-Mart and Cifra

Having risen steadily through the 1970s and 1980s to surpass Sears, Roebuck and become the dominant retailer in the United States, by the early 1990s Wal-Mart was looking for opportunities abroad. "I don't know if Wal-Mart can truly maintain its leadership position by just staying in this country," Sam Walton, Wal-Mart's founder, said in his 1992 biography, *Made in America.*

But "absorbing people from other cultures quickly and smoothly into the company will present a real challenge," Walton noted. So to smooth the way, Wal-Mart searched for partners, first in Mexico, then elsewhere in Latin America. Wal-Mart found an ideal partner in Cifra, Mexico's largest retailer. Both Wal-Mart and Cifra were family-led retailers, each the biggest in its market, each innovative and comfortable with technology, each extremely cost-conscious and willing to trade lower margins for market share. As well as a smooth fit for the businesses, the alliance was a comfortable fit culturally.

Wal-Mart was founded in 1950 when Sam Walton moved to Bentonville, Arkansas, and opened a Walton 5&10 store. In 1962, he and his brother opened the first Wal-Mart Discount City. They took the company public in 1970, and the Walton family continues to control about 40 percent of the stock.

Cifra was founded in 1958, in Mexico City, by Jeronimo Arango and his brothers. According to Arango, he was visiting New York City when he saw shoppers lined up, waiting for an E. J. Korvette discount department store to open. He phoned his brothers on the spot and proposed the new business. It eventually grew into the second-largest publicly owned company in Mexico, after Téléfonos de Mexico.

If Wal-Mart needed new fronts abroad on which it could grow, Cifra, like other Mexican retailers, also felt a strong need to partner. "We knew the large U.S. chains would come to Mexico once the North American Free Trade Agreement was signed," one Cifra executive told the November 23, 1994, *Financial Times*. "To survive we had to become as competitive and efficient as the largest U.S. retailers." Until 1986, when Mexico joined the General Agreement on Tariffs and Trade (now the World Trade Organization), Mexicans who wanted foreign goods generally had to visit shopping malls outside the borders. With increased free trade, imported goods became widely available as foreign shops opened in major Mexican cities. Nafta greatly increased the momentum.

Cifra and its domestic competitors, as well as Wal-Mart and other retailing giants abroad, expected Mexico to offer enormous growth opportunities for a number of reasons:

- It had not yet benefited from the leverage with suppliers that larger operations bring.
- Average income in Mexico was rising steadily and approaching the point where consumer spending was likely to accelerate.
- Half the population was under nineteen years old.
- Mexico was believed to be underretailed, even in Mexico City. In 1993, for example, a study by Baring Securities found that supermarkets in Mexico had only one-tenth the floor space per customer of those in Europe.

And their expectations were generally met. With the arrival of free trade and the opening of the Mexican economy, retail sales surged.

As well as a chance to grow, Wal-Mart and Cifra each saw in the alliance an opportunity to learn. For Wal-Mart, Cifra would provide lessons in how to serve Latin markets, and if the lessons were learned well, Wal-Mart could take those lessons to Brazil, Argentina, and elsewhere. For Cifra, the alliance was an opportunity to learn from the inside how the most efficient and profitable retailer in the world organized and conducted its business.

The alliance "allowed us to install well-proven systems and programs which Wal-Mart already has in operation," Henry Davis, the president of Cifra, pointed out to the *Financial Times*. "We are, therefore, reducing our costs and eliminating the risk of failure." Cifra executives said they learned from Wal-Mart how to manage the growth of their operations, particularly how to expand wholesale operations and distributions centers.

From the early days of the alliance, Wal-Mart and Cifra agreed to jointly and exclusively pursue operational synergies in distribution, purchasing, information technology, business systems, point-of-sale merchandising, and so forth, learning from each other and adopting the best format and management processes of each. "We shared our capabilities," said Jaime Escandon, Cifra's treasurer, in an interview: "Wal-Mart's IT [information technology] and process technology, inventory control systems, distribution know-how; Cifra's merchandising skill, employee and customer understanding, purchasing skill, site selection, and inflation management." It was also agreed, from the early days, that Wal-Mart might eventually purchase a substantial equity position in Cifra if the partnership proved to be successful for both partners.

It was 1991 when Wal-Mart and Cifra signed their first alliance agreement, involving one pilot store. The agreement also allowed either party to walk away after three years. But in fact the opposite occurred: Wal-Mart and Cifra steadily expanded the scope of their alliance. In May 1992, the alliance was expanded, with the companies agreeing to act as equal partners for all new stores opened in Mexico. At the time, Wal-Mart had 1,735 Wal-Mart stores (including 9 supercenters), 215 Sam's Club warehouses, and 4 Hypermarts in the United States. In Mexico, Cifra owned 38 Bodega Aurrea discount stores; 35 Superma, 2 Gran Basar, and 28 Suburbia stores, and 72 Vips restaurants.

These existing Mexican stores remained under Cifra's ownership and control. From 1992 to 1996, Wal-Mart and Cifra each put nearly $1 billion in cash into the alliance, and by 1997, the alliance had 145 stores and 20,000 employees. Then Wal-Mart and Cifra decided to take the partnership to a different level. In 1997, all the stores operated by the alliance were merged into Cifra, and Wal-Mart agreed to pay $1.2 billion for 46 percent of Cifra's common stock. "This is a very good marriage," said Les Copeland, senior manager of international corporate affairs at Wal-Mart.

In almost every way, said Escandon, the alliance has proven an unqualified success. Even during the worst fiscal crisis in Mexican history, when the peso collapsed in 1994 and dragged down with it Mexico's stock market during much of 1995, Cifra's share price remained buoyant.

Within Mexico, Cifra has firmly established itself as the top mass retailer. And Wal-Mart has taken many of the lessons it has learned in Mexico and applied them in Brazil and elsewhere in Latin America.

Hewlett-Packard and Canon

Hewlett-Packard is, of course, one of the two hallowed "garage" stories in Silicon Valley (the other being Apple). It was founded in 1938 in a Palo Alto garage by William Hewlett and David Packard (two Stanford-trained engineers), and its first product was an audio oscillator. Hewlett and Packard were able to persuade Walt Disney Studios to buy eight of the devices, which were used to help create the animated film *Fantasia*. In 1959, Hewlett-Packard pushed outside the United States, creating operations in Switzerland and Germany. In 1972, it introduced the hand-held scientific calculator. Today, it ranks among the top ten companies in the world in the sale of desktop computers, printers, and network servers, as well as being a leader in systems integration, programming and testing, and medical equipment.

However, for a good long while, this technology giant insisted on developing all its own technology. So concerned was management with controlling its own fate that HP even manufactured all the screws it needed for its hardware. But with globalization and growing competition, HP realized it had to change its philosophy.

"I think it's impossible, even for a company of HP's size, to have competence in every area," CEO Lew Platt said in 1994. "It is very important to find alliance partners" ("Technology Leader of the Year," *Industry Week,* Jan. 9, 1995). So over the years, HP "redefined" its "notions of innovation to include leveraging technology developed outside of" the company. During that time, HP has also formed many alliances, none more striking or strategic than the partnership formed in the 1970s with Canon Inc., which agreed to develop and provide the engines that would power HP's market-dominating laser printers.

When the first laser printers were created in the mid-1970s by International Business Machines and Xerox, they were enormous—and enormously expensive, with prices in the hundreds of thousands of dollars—powerful machines intended to serve the corporate market. In developing its own laser printers, Hewlett-Packard was quick to see the advantages of working with Canon (and so was Apple Computer). And by 1979, Canon had developed laser technology similar to that now used in CD players and had come up with a way to make a simple printer. Far slower than the huge corporate models, capable of printing only a few pages a minute, the new printer sold for $3,500. The combination of relatively low price and laser quality found a huge market among small businesses and professionals working at home.

Even at that time, neither company was a stranger to alliances. Canon, from its Tokyo base, had forged alliances whose goal was to wed Canon technology to other firms' commercial capabilities. Through this alliance strategy, Canon had achieved enormous growth. In 1981, for example, it was roughly the same size as Nikon. By leveraging its capabilities through a spread of alliances, Canon grew to four times Nikon's size in less than a decade. Yet for a long time the company had remained quintessentially Japanese. Founded in 1933 by Takeshi Mitarai and Saburo Uchida, and known at the time as Seiki Kogaku Kenkyusho, Canon was the first Japanese company to create a 35-millimeter camera. It was called the Kwanon, then later the Canon, and the company took that brand name as its own name. Then, while retaining its strong position in photography, Canon developed a far larger and more profitable business, with a wide variety of business machines—notably copiers, printers, facsimile machines, and computer systems. It also became a significant producer of machines for semiconductor manufacturing and medical treatment. It was in order to grow those businesses that Canon determined that it had to look abroad.

"Seeking partners in Japan is futile," said Canon's senior managing director at the time, Hiroshi Tanaka. "Silicon Valley is ten years, maybe twenty years, ahead of anywhere else. America is unmatched in every area of computer hardware and software" ("In the Digital Derby, There's No Inside Lane," *Business Week,* Nov. 18, 1994).

For Hewlett-Packard too, the HP–Canon alliance, engineered by John Young, Platt's predecessor as CEO, followed a string of other alliances: with Hitachi (for precision architecture chip technology), Yokogawa (logic systems), Northern Telecom (microprocessor development systems), Sony (digital audio tapes), Arthur Andersen (management consulting on computer-integrated manufacturing)—and Canon, for "smart" typewriters.

As the laser alliance was constructed, Canon provided the engine that, in effect, spurts the toner onto the page. HP provided the software and microprocessors that oversee engine operations. HP was also responsible for marketing the printers. "Our core competence is in packaging and putting in the format or electronics that cause those engines to perform well, and then doing the sales and marketing," said Platt. "So that's an example of finding a partner with complementary core strengths."

The alliance served each partner well. Hewlett-Packard gained a reliable, sophisticated source of essential technology for considerably less than it would have spent developing the engine on its own. For Canon, the alliance (and a similar partnership with Apple Computer to provide Macintosh-compatible printers) provided a means to grow its market and dominate the field far beyond what it could have achieved through selling only its own brand-name printers.

Nevertheless the Canon and Hewlett-Packard alliance brought together fierce technological rivals. Even through the long years of the laser printer engine alliance, Canon and HP continued to compete vigorously in the markets for laser printers, color ink-jet printers, and more.

For example, the alliance led to HP's LaserJet line, which quickly attracted a strong following. Canon then brought out a laser printer with the same engine. And the Canon printer offered an additional feature at no extra cost—infinitely scalable fonts. HP was forced to respond with a similar feature, to the benefit of its customers.

One impetus for HP's commitment to alliances was the extent to which IBM dominated high technology in the 1960s and 1970s. Much as technology companies today go to great lengths to avoid domination by Microsoft and Intel, so did technology companies then motivate themselves to take on the Big Blue behemoth. Alliances were an important part of this strategy. "We would not have such a successful laser printer business if we didn't have a strong alliance with Canon," Platt said. "We counted on them to be the world's best producer of laser print engines.

"Once the world was simple, and so were relationships," he continued. "Your partners were your allies, and your competitors were your foes. Today, people we compete with one day are our partners the next. Alliances are critical. We can't do everything ourselves."

Chapter 5
The Eight-Step Roadmap

A disciplined approach is critical in propelling a company to superior alliance results and avoiding the pitfalls that ensnare inexperienced managers. Through our research and experience with clients around the globe, we have created a battle-tested methodology for alliance formation. It reflects one striking finding of our research: non-U.S. companies often have a broader vision of what an alliance can achieve. They see an alliance with a company in the United States as a gateway or launching pad for ever-greater collaboration, while their U.S. counterparts seem more focused on a single business opportunity.

As we noted in Chapter Three, our approach takes the four stages of alliance formation—identification, valuation, negotiation, and implementation—and breaks them into eight practical and actionable steps (see Exhibit 5.1). Each step contains an associated set of best practices, the practices that help explain the successes of some companies and the disappointments of others. Chapter Three presented seven of the most important best practices. In this chapter, we discuss what occurs in each step of alliance formation and the kinds of best practices each step typically calls for, and we close with a checklist for boards of directors.

Exhibit 5.1. Follow a Roadmap to Alliance Success

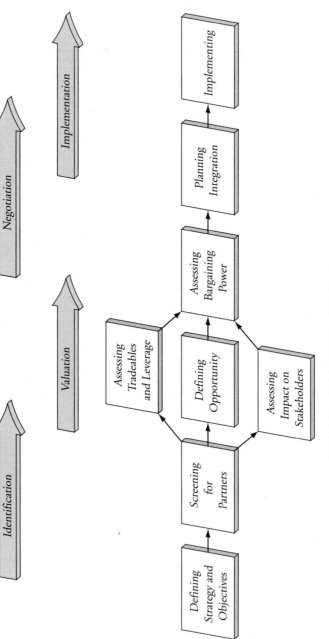

Identification

Valuation

Negotiation

Implementation

Defining Strategy and Objectives

Screening for Partners

Assessing Tradeables and Leverage

Defining Opportunity

Assessing Impact on Stakeholders

Assessing Bargaining Power

Planning Integration

Implementing

ALLIANCE FORMATION METHODOLOGY

Identifying Best Practices

After we surveyed more than five hundred major corporations in the United States and abroad and identified the specific activities that distinguish experienced firms from less-experienced firms, we then asked each company to rate its skill level for each best practice, from 1, relatively undeveloped skills; up through 4, expert skills; to 5, world-class skills. We came up with both an overall determination of the most effective best practices and a similar analysis by industry. For comparison and to focus specifically on differentiators that lead to success, we then established two groups. The first, "companies experienced in strategic alliances," we defined as having done at least nine alliances—in many cases far more—while realizing at least a 25 percent return on investment. The second group, "relative novices," are companies that have done only one or two alliances, with a return on investment of less than 10 percent.

We also analyzed the success rate for alliances, contrasting companies that did many alliances, earned high returns, and were enthusiastic about alliance activity with those that viewed themselves as less successful and that hence were less enthusiastic. We asked each respondent to measure success against the company's own objectives, using whatever criteria he or she believed to be the relevant metrics. This is important because there are many different reasons for engaging in alliances.

From these findings we were able to isolate the best practices with the greatest spread in skills. The one hundred best practices that we identified have been incorporated into our alliance formation methodology. Each of the eight steps, or activities, in the methodology (discussed in detail below) is broken down into best practices, and associated with each practice is a description of the five skill levels. The complete set of one hundred best practices and the associated skill levels is a proprietary tool that Booz·Allen uses with its clients, but let us consider here a few examples of diagnosing a company's use of best practices. Exhibit 5.2 shows an overall framework for looking at best practices against the steps in the alliance formation process to determine skill levels. Exhibit 5.3 is a sample

Exhibit 5.2. Diagnose Skill Levels of Best Practices for Each Activity

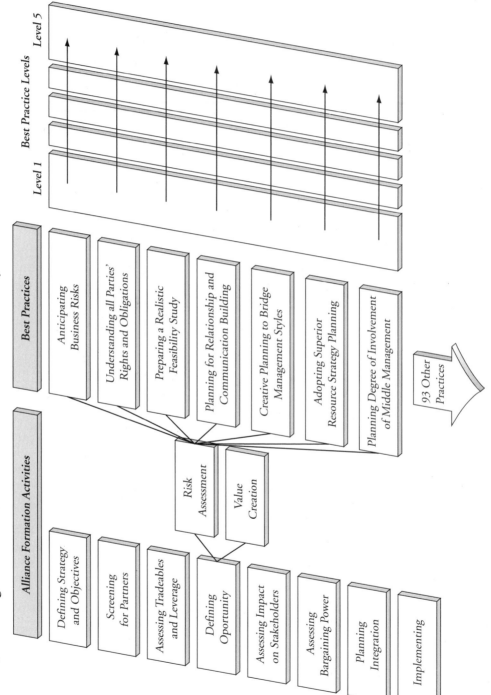

Exhibit 5.3. Sample Best Practice Template

— Increasing Sophistication →

Best Practice	Other Widespread Practices			Current Best Practice	Future Best Practice
	Level 1	Level 2	Level 3	Level 4	Level 5
Anticipating Business Risks	General statement of risks to alliance	Clear statement and probability of alliance success	Statement of alliance impact on other domestic business	Statement of alliance impact on other international businesses	Statement of alliance impact on future attractive opportunities
Understanding all Parties' Rights and Obligations	Vague rights and obligations	Better understanding of rights, not obligations	Description of rights and obligations, but not understood by partner	Description of rights and obligations, but requires court arbitration	Description of rights and obligations clearly understood by all partners
Preparing a Realistic Feasibility Study	No independent analysis—control by corporate staff	Limited operational analysis (ad hoc stage)	Operational analysis limited in tactical emphasis	Balance between corporate definition and operational and tactical know-how	Partners share plans, assumptions and analysis

Importance to Business Performance	Average Level Achieved	Level of Best Competitors
Rating (1 to 5)		

template for several of the one hundred practices, and Exhibit 5.4 is a sample output, comparing the assessment to external benchmarks.

For example, the first best practice in Exhibit 5.3 is anticipating business risks. The template then defines five possible outcomes of applying this best practice, each one representing a skill level. The outcomes range from simply preparing a general statement of risks to alliances to preparing a specific statement on the impact of the alliance on future attractive opportunities.

The relevant best practices vary significantly from industry to industry. However, to help managers compare their current practices against those of companies that have achieved superior alliance results in general, we have developed the self-diagnostic exercise shown in Exhibit 5.5. If your total score on this exercise is 8 to 20, your company may have done a couple of alliances, but you have not been happy with the results. If your score is more than 20 but less than 44, you probably have had some alliance success but have not achieved the high ROE and ROI of the most successful alliance companies. If your score is above 44, you have learned the lessons of alliance building, though you

Exhibit 5.4. Sample Best Practice Template for Human Resources

Best Practice	Other Widespread Practices			Current Best Practice	World Best Practice
	Level 1	Level 2	Level 3	Level 4	Level 5
Creative Planning to Bridge Management Styles of Partners	No plan to bridge partner's management style in alliance	Knowledge of partner's management style and culture, little understanding of impact on alliance	Executive profiles, organizational structure, cultural and working environment, reward and promotion programs matched with alliance needs and priorities	Interactive planning highlighting partners' organizational structure, cultural and working environment, reward and promotion programs compared to alliance needs and priorities	Statement of alliance impact on future attractive opportunities
Example/ client		X			
All industries	50%	20%	20%	10%	

Low ... High

Best practice importance					X

Exhibit 5.5. Test Your Company's Capabilities

Rate your company's capability to perform each step, using the following scale:

Very weak	Weak	Somewhat weak	Adequate	Somewhat strong	Strong	Very Strong
1	2	3	4	5	6	7

Capability to Perform Alliance Formation Steps	*Rating*
1. Capability to define strategy and objectives	_____
2. Capability to screen for partners (identify and prioritize)	_____
3. Capability to assess tradeables and leverage	_____
4. Capability to define opportunity (and analyze it)	_____
5. Capability to assess the impact on stakeholders	_____
6. Capability to assess bargaining power	_____
7. Capability to plan integration	_____
8. Capability to implement	_____
TOTAL SCORE	_____

can certainly still improve. (Note, too, that European and Asian executives, whose companies typically score above 44, say they find many Americans overrate their companies' capabilities on these steps.)

The Eight Activities

Let's return now to the roadmap to alliance success and examine each of its steps.

Step 1: Defining Strategy and Objectives

Companies experienced in alliances take time to determine what it is they are looking for:

- They reach a clear consensus on why the firm cannot succeed on its own, including why alliances can fill capability gaps better than in-house development or acquisition.
- They know where value is generated by an alliance—and why each partner cannot realize that value effectively on its own.
- They study the resource requirements and assess whether they have the motivation and the predisposition to deliver those resources.
- They identify the important market characteristics and drivers and the role that alliances can play in preparing them to meet those market drivers.
- They understand their key capability gaps against the full range of requirements, particularly in alliances formed to pursue new markets. They know that an alliance can fill some capability gaps but that many alliances fail because other important gaps were not addressed.

Over time the drivers and objectives that motivate a company can of course change, so corporate strategy must evolve. Drivers are generally industry dependent, shaped by the characteristics of an industry (see Exhibit 5.6).

The telecommunications industry, for example, can be thought of as capital intensive, highly technological, mature, nationally and locally based, and offering commodity-like products. In the 1980s, industry drivers were growth, diversification, and regulatory freedom. By the early 1990s, the drivers had shifted to vertical integration, market access, and global presence. Now they are shifting once more, with strategic fit, market access, and complementary capabilities emerging as the most important drivers.

MCI Communication, for example, before it became the target of competing takeover offers in 1997 and eventually agreed to be acquired by Worldcom, had developed an alliance with Microsoft and Digital Equipment that was driven by a desire for market access and strategic fit. The three companies sought to develop an integrated package of communication services and products that would allow any firm's employees to collaborate even when based at different locations. It would have been an *intranet.* MCI contributed its network connections to the

Exhibit 5.6. Drivers Emanate from Industry Characteristics: Telecommunications Example

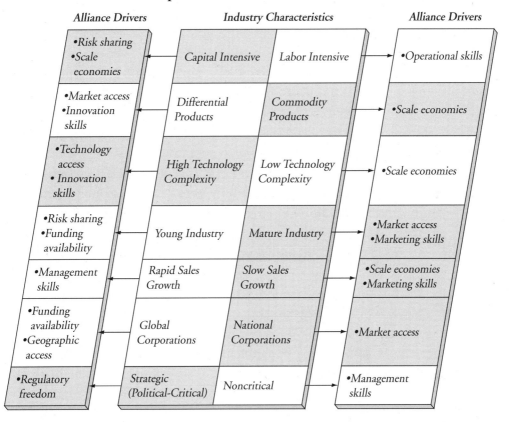

Alliance Drivers	Industry Characteristics		Alliance Drivers
•Risk sharing •Scale economies	Capital Intensive	Labor Intensive	•Operational skills
•Market access •Innovation skills	Differential Products	Commodity Products	•Scale economies
•Technology access •Innovation skills	High Technology Complexity	Low Technology Complexity	•Scale economies
•Risk sharing •Funding availability	Young Industry	Mature Industry	•Market access •Marketing skills
•Management skills	Rapid Sales Growth	Slow Sales Growth	•Scale economies •Marketing skills
•Funding availability •Geographic access	Global Corporations	National Corporations	•Market access
•Regulatory freedom	Strategic (Political-Critical)	Noncritical	•Management skills

☐ *Telecommunications industry chararcteristics*

alliance, Digital its experience in installing and managing large data networks, and Microsoft its expertise in software, including its Windows NT operating system and its messaging programs. This integrated intranet package would have also allowed internal posting of marketing and product information as well as details of employee benefits. The partners expected intranet sales to bring a billion dollars in annual revenue.

Too much emphasis cannot be given to the importance of rigorous evaluation in defining strategy and objectives. The most successful alliance companies have learned that an ad hoc or soft evaluation places an alliance in a precarious position from the start.

Step 2: Screening for Partners

Screening, identifying, and approaching partners is one of the most difficult hurdles in alliance building. Successful managers say the most important best practice in this process is to take an active rather than an reactive stance. This is difficult, the managers say, but essential if a company is to avoid repeated fire-drill routines, spending time and resources responding to overtures from other companies. An active posture enables a company to screen out unsuitable partners and to study at length the strengths of prospective partners and the options that different partner choices would offer. An explicit fit analysis should go beyond potential partners' capabilities and their industry and market positions to include their cultural fit. One factor that should be examined closely is the prospective partners' alliance histories.

As part of this screening process, managers should articulate the alliance drivers—the benefits anticipated—for both their company and the prospective partner companies as well (see Exhibit 5.7). Most alliance partners have complementary drivers, but that does not mean that these drivers are the same. Taking each partner's needs into account helps build trust and starts the relationship building and the bargaining on a solid basis. Anticipating each partner's reactions and being able to see things from that partner's perspective can help keep lines of communication open when difficulties arise.

Step 3: Assessing Tradeables and Leverage

By assessing tradeables and leverage, potential partners determine just what they have to offer and what they stand to gain. The process involves

- Assessing which capabilities have the potential to be differential in the alliance.
- Defining what is deliverable, by whom, and how the alliance ownership will be divided between the partners—whether equity or nonequity stakes are involved.
- Understanding the potential advantage of the alliance's products over existing products; examining things from the customers' perspective.

Exhibit 5.7. Understand Alliance Drivers from
Both Partners' Perspectives

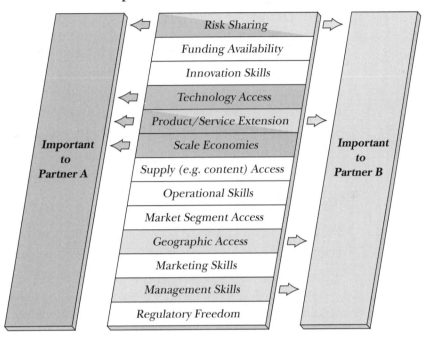

- Quantifying value creation and its source. A striking number of
  alliances are not successfully negotiated because the parties fail to
  be explicit at the start on how to determine the value created by
  the alliance beyond what the partners might have done on their
  own. Failure to agree on this point can sabotage the alliance.
- Acknowledging whatever *dis*advantages might accrue under the
  alliance, so that surprises can be avoided and disappointments dealt
  with in a professional rather than an emotional manner.

In one tradeables analysis, each partner determines which capabilities are critical to the alliance and then assesses its own capability position. Another approach is to lay out the alliance drivers and then
identify the relative contributions each partner can make. Microsoft,
Intel, and General Instruments took that approach when they formed

a partnership to link the cable television converter box that sits atop most television sets with an *information gateway* into the realm of computing and cyberspace. General Instruments brought to the alliance considerable expertise and market share in converter boxes as well as skills in encryption and compression. Intel provided the microprocessor; Microsoft, the software. Development funding and risks were shared by all three partners. Their alliance is a model of how each company, acting in its own interest, tried to create a fair and equitable arrangement that would stand the test of time and yield increased value and rewards from the marketplace.

Step 4: Defining Opportunity

Even when pursuing markets outside their traditional strongholds, it is remarkable how many companies rely on superficial analysis. Often, we have found, the alliance feasibility study seems more dependent on faith than on analysis. The most common failing is in gauging the likely reaction of competitors, customers, and other stakeholders. As companies depend increasingly on alliances for growth and revenue generation, this issue will become more and more important. From a process perspective, quantifying the size of the opportunity is essential to successful negotiation and implementation of an alliance. Too many negotiators fail to define crisply the magnitude of the opportunity, and consequently they lose the chance to use it as the lubricant to keep the negotiations moving through the inevitable rough spots. And the reverse may occur as well. Some negotiators fail to determine that the opportunity may be quite limited and not worth the effort.

The steps needed to assess an opportunity vary from industry to industry and from market to market. To address this hurdle, Booz·Allen developed Dynamic Alliance Simulation, which grew out of war-gaming for military contractors. It creates a customized simulation of a client's business, so that managers can live through an alliance negotiation and, along the way, gain a better understanding of strategy dynamics. The simulation also helps a newly formed alliance team bond and develop common points of reference.

Step 5: Assessing Impact on Stakeholders

A thorough assessment of all stakeholders' concerns is an essential step in alliance building. The assessment should be broad, covering not just the concerns of the obvious parties—investors, workers, suppliers, customers—but also of unions and regulatory officials. (Alliances have generally not received the close regulatory scrutiny that acquisitions have, but that may well change. Note the intense scrutiny on both sides of the Atlantic of the broad alliance proposed by British Airways and American Airlines.) The assessment should also consider what might be done to alleviate whatever concerns are identified.

How investors perceive alliances can be hard to calculate. On any given day when an alliance is announced, share prices will be influenced by many other factors as well, from broad economic news and general market moves to investment analysts' recommendations. In 1995, Tarun Khanna of the Harvard Business School and Bharat Anand of Yale studied one thousand alliances formed since 1990 to try to isolate how the stock market values alliances. They concluded that alliances do create value and also that the stock market reacts differently to different types of alliances. Licensing agreements are valued the most, they found, followed by market and research-and-development alliances.

On the day British Petroleum and Mobil announced their alliance, their combined market value shot up a stunning $5.8 billion! When Merck and Rhône-Poulenc Rorer announced an alliance, $5.4 billion in value was created. And on the day when the Walt Disney Company announced an alliance with Pixar, Steven Jobs's company, which created the animation for the film *Toy Story,* the stock market pushed up Disney's share price 3 percent and Pixar's 49 percent, resulting in value creation of $438 million.

Joint ventures were greeted less enthusiastically by investors than were other types of alliances, though the reaction varied sharply from one industry to another. In high-technology industries, the study found, investors prefer tight, equity-bound structures that give the alliance partners close control over the technology; in pharmaceuticals, investors seem to prefer looser contractual arrangements. "I would recommend establishing a structure within the parent company that forces management to take the shareholders' interests into account when it forms a new alliance," Tarun Khanna said in an interview in the *Alliance Analyst* newsletter. The executive in charge of alliance activities should "face pressure to take the shareholders' interests into account."

Step 6: Assessing Bargaining Power

Five best practices stand above all others when a company undertakes an assessment of its bargaining power:

- Clearly defining the contribution of key capabilities and resources needed to make an alliance successful
- Protecting the company's core resources and making clear to a prospective partner what these are and why you are protecting them
- Studying a prospective partner's negotiating style and history by analyzing other alliances that the company has entered into
- Knowing why the other company is at the table—what strategic and nonstrategic benefits it seeks
- Making judgments on the type of and depth of resources and commitment that the prospective partner will bring to the alliance

One bargaining framework that many successful companies use assesses what core capability is critical or noncritical to current business and whether the company has an advantaged or disadvantaged position. After the analysis, the company can decide its method of capability procurement—that is, whether acquisition, internal development, or alignment is likely to be most effective. The same analysis is helpful when a company confronted with a new business opportunity must secure gap-filling skills. After the analysis, managers should be much clearer on which option is best to employ because they should have a realistic understanding of their company's position.

The company is then ready to negotiate effectively, which is a complex process. We recommend that the uninitiated seek help. Even the basic ground rules are a bit complex. In negotiating the agreement, the most successful alliance-building companies use a two-track approach, especially when the alliance involves equity.

On track one, senior managers approach a potential partner and, in a cordial and unthreatening way, outline the proposed alliance's strategy and goals. They sketch the forms of cooperation that may be acceptable, and they describe in general terms the resource contributions that will be needed. From these initial contacts, the senior managers should be able to determine the level of acceptance and depth of commitment the prospective partner is willing to give to the arrangement. One easy way to stumble at this point is to overestimate the other party's commitment, which can lead to unclear objectives and goals. Correctly understanding commitment is particularly important when the potential partners are competitors, because alliances often move into markets that compete with the partners' separate operations. This occurrence can create hostility and tension if it is not anticipated during negotiations.

Once a comfort zone between senior managers has been established, the alliance partners should prepare a memorandum of understanding that provides a framework for track two, the more detailed discussions by operational and functional alliance planning teams. Everyone on the track two team needs to be clear on the strategy and goals of the alliance because these teams plan alliance details and estimate the chances of success. The discussions should cover the alliance structure, partner resource contribution levels, financial requirements, and technology inputs.

Each company should also be aware of any other alliance arrangements in which the other companies are involved, in case restrictions previously negotiated hinder the alliance under discussion. Years ago, Paramount Communications and Warner Brothers struck an alliance that they hoped would solve the advertising problems each had with its cable television systems. To attract national advertising by major companies, cable systems needed to demonstrate that they reached 70 percent of households in the United States. Paramount and Warner each had systems that reached about 40 percent of households, and this forced them to rely on local and regional advertising, which was less lucrative. But as each company focused on what the alliance could bring to it, it also failed to tell the other that existing alliances with other companies prohibited the very deal the two were negotiating. Warner, for instance, had an alliance with WGN, a television station in Chicago, and with WGN's parent, the Tribune Company, that barred Warner from investing in another company that created programming. Paramount had an alliance with Chris-Craft, an owner of broadcast stations, which stipulated that Paramount could not invest in a competing network. When Chris-Craft and the Tribune Company learned of the intended alliance, they immediately insisted on compliance with the restrictive terms of their own deals—to the dismay of Warner and Paramount.

We suggest that the guiding memorandum of understanding be in effect for a limited period of time, to create some urgency among the track two team members to work out the details. Once the cooperative planning effort is completed, real negotiations can begin among track one participants.

Regional and cultural experts should be on these track one negotiating teams, and senior managers should be kept up-to-date on events. It is also essential that all participants agree on how much power the chief negotiator on each side wields. All parties to the talks should also have a full understanding of the minimum and maximum levels of commitment that will be necessary—in capital, technology, and personnel. Specifically, the operating arrangement, timetables, goals, and performance measures should be discussed at this level. Finally, the negotiating teams should be empowered to walk away from the deal if they sense it will not work.

That is a lot to contemplate. Here is a checklist of what any agreement should include:

- Clear objectives and defined levels of commitment
- An organizational structure that fits the alliance strategy; rewards that reflect the risks that alliance employees assume
- Investment and compensation rewards tied to clear performance measures; clearly defined benchmarks that the alliance will be measured against
- Finance, tax, and legal considerations

- Detailed penalty, arbitration, and divorce clauses; specification of level and degree of support necessary should the alliance dissolve
- Provisions to renew the commitment to the alliance
- Formulas for transfer pricing, earnings, and equity clearly defined and linked to resource and capability contribution
- An alliance board of directors reflecting the resource contribution of each partner (remembering that equity formulas often do not reflect each partner's ownership or influence in an alliance)
- A formula for tallying asset and capabilities contributions (keeping a rolling tally of contributions and benefits)
- The ability to accommodate changes

Step 7: Planning Integration

Planning integration, that is, doing the planning to make the partners' capabilities function together, is not only a critical area in alliance planning, it is also an area where European and Asian executives believe U.S. companies could improve. Experienced companies place heavy emphasis on planning integration in order to get the alliance off to a fast start. Among the best practices they rely on are

- Structuring the alliance to meet the needs of the alliance rather than those of the partners
- Assigning high-caliber managers to the alliance and coupling pay and investment to results
- Rigorously linking strategic objectives to budgets and resources, adopting a periodic review process, and fixing the authority and responsibilities of the managers
- Clearly defining divorce procedures, penalties, and exit obligations

The selection of the right kind of manager is an often overlooked yet critical element of the alliance-building process. If the alliance's goal, for example, is to create a new market by integrating the capabilities of the partners, the operating manager should have entrepreneurial characteristics—being a change handler who can exhibit confidence and be buoyant about possibilities and who has training as a risk analyzer. Alternatively, an alliance focused on gaining major efficiencies should have as its manager a process analyzer who is control oriented and a management driver (see Exhibit 5.8).

The approach to recruiting and compensating and also the traits and styles desirable in the senior management team need to be adapted to accord with the alliance focus (see Exhibit 5.9). An alliance intended to create a new market needs energetic traits and a willingness to experiment brought together by intelligence and common sense and by incentives oriented to growth. For an alliance intended to gain major efficiencies, the appropriate traits are investigative and challenging, the style analytical, executed by a seasoned team, with incentives that are results based.

Compensation particularly needs to be tailored to the alliance objectives (see Exhibit 5.10). If the alliance strategy is directed at creating new markets, compensation should be focused on the future payout and tied to strategic objectives, not to the large yearly bonus that makes sense where gaining major efficiencies is the primary goal. Many companies make the mistake of imposing their existing compensation program on the alliance. That does not take into account either the risks or the objectives of the alliance.

Exhibit 5.8. Select the Right Kind of Manager

Manager Selection		
Alliance Focus	Operating Manager	Characteristics
Create new market by integrating capabilities	Intrapreneurial	Change handler Confident Risk analyzer
Grow share by raising competitive barriers	Sophisticated	Discriminator Experienced Value analyzer
Gain major efficiencies	Evaluator	Process analyzer Control oriented Measurement driven

Exhibit 5.9.   Tailor the Senior Management Team to the Requirements

Management Team Selection				
Alliance Focus	Recruit	Compensation	Trait	Style
Create new market	Intelligence Common sense	Growth oriented	Energetic	Experimental
Grow share barriers	Experience Rational ability	Competitive enhancement	Innovative	Value focused
Gain major efficiencies	Skills Seasonedness	Results based	Investigative	Analytical

Exhibit 5.10.   Tailor Compensation to Objectives

Management Compensation and Bonuses		
Alliance Focus	Yearly Results	Future Payout
Create new market by integrating capabilities	Salary, small bonus	Phantom stock or balloon reward based on business size
Grow share by raising competitive barriers	Salary, medium bonus	Medium cash reward based on value enhancement
Gain major efficiencies	Salary, major bonus	Some cash reward based on impact of efficiencies

Step 8: Implementing

Once a battle-tested senior executive said to us, "I will always take a first-rate implementation plan and a good strategy over a second-rate implementation plan and a first-rate strategy. Why? Because we know how to adjust and learn as we go forward—but if we can't implement, what good is strategy?"

That philosophy applies to alliances as well. By its very nature, an alliance requires a flexible and lean management style. An alliance must have a structure based on the challenges it faces. It needs to be nurtured. This means it must have available measurement tools and timetables that will help managers locate the difficulties to resolve as well as the opportunities to take advantage of. Among the best practices that successful companies use when they implement alliances are these:

- Creating a flexible and lean organizational structure
- Basing alliance structure and processes on alliance strategy and requirements rather than partners' strategies and requirements
- Tracking competitors' reactions to the alliance along with tracking the progress of the alliance itself
- Preparing detailed timetables and measurement tools, with periodic review
- Relying on open communication to provide flexibility in resolving issues rather than turning only to the original alliance agreement for guidance

European and Asian executives put a particular emphasis on three additional best practices: defining early the management roles, providing managers the power needed to accomplish goals, and making lessons learned anywhere in the alliance available across the alliance on a real-time basis. The Europeans and Asians find that most of their U.S. counterparts still need to master these three important best practices.

Directors' Concerns

The methodology presented in this chapter provides a roadmap for managers and executives. Yet alliance issues are weighty, as are the stakes for each company involved. So before giving a green light to an alliance, the board of directors of each partner should run through the following additional checklist of concerns:

- Degree of cross-industry skill transfer—*Are we creating a new competitor with access to core skills?*

- Alteration of competitive position—*Will the alliance affect the competitive position of our other businesses?*
- Scope of legal liabilities—*Where, who might be affected, and what size might the liability be?*
- Effect on stakeholders—*How will banks, investors, funds, employees, customers, suppliers, and unions feel about the alliance?*
- Range of governance and control—*Who is accountable, who has authority, and who has responsibility?*
- Degree of obligations and rights—*What are the penalties, the rights, and the arbitration and divorce procedures?*
- Impact on the organization—*What will be the impact on the parent company from alliance compensation, structure, rewards, and degree of loyalty?*

The directors should be closely involved in any alliance that is likely to have high impact on their company and that taps core capabilities. Involvement is less essential when impact is limited and core capabilities are not involved.

The roadmap and best practices presented in this chapter can help a company inexperienced in alliance activities achieve the superior returns characteristic of more experienced companies. Through a disciplined approach, a company can fill critical capability gaps and enhance its competitive position within the realities of its resource constraints. By leveraging existing resources and avoiding incremental investment, alliances allow a company to build differential capabilities in more areas than it has time or resources to develop.

For a wide variety of reasons, European and Asian companies were quickest to see the benefits and to use alliances to their great advantage. In the following chapter we examine their histories, activities, and perspectives and also take a look at some of the fast-growing markets in Asia and Latin America.

Chapter 6
Lessons and Opportunities Across Borders
The View from Outside the United States

Companies in the United States are quickly moving up the alliance ladder, but they have yet to attain the levels of experience of many European and Asian counterparts. As we pointed out earlier, sales from the average strategic alliance in the United States are $80 million annually, far less than the European average of $250 million. However, that is not very surprising, given that alliance investment by the top one thousand U.S. companies averages $40 million, whereas European companies average $150 million. Moreover, in the United States the average life span of an alliance has been ten years; in Europe it has been fifteen, and in Japan twenty.

Yet U.S. investment in alliances has doubled in the last five years and is likely to continue to grow. Other regions are also rapidly expanding their alliance activity. In Latin America, Russia, Eastern Europe, and India, the spread of democracy and free enterprise has allowed corporations to chart their own courses. Their enthusiasm for and accessibility to foreign partners has led to a spurt of alliance activity (see Exhibit 6.1).

In this chapter the section on Latin America was written by Wouter Rosingh and Artur Ribeiro Neto; the section on Asia by Doug Ng, Ian Buchanon, Gerry Komlofske, and Kevin Jones; and the section on Europe by Alex Gneisenau.

**Exhibit 6.1.   Non-U.S. Companies Are Using
Strategic Alliances as Key Strategic Options**

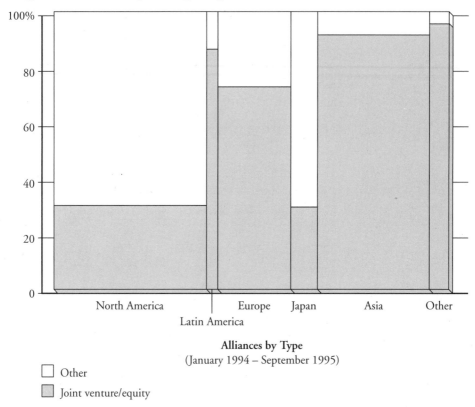

Alliances by Type
(January 1994 – September 1995)

☐ Other

▨ Joint venture/equity

Source: Strategic Data Corporation; Booz·Allen & Hamilton analysis.

The worldwide interest in alliance building offers major opportunities for growth to companies that understand cross-border alliance building. In addition, the experience of European and Asian executives has given them some useful views on specific ways in which U.S. companies can increase their desirability as alliance partners. The following pages outline these opportunities and views and some helpful history.

Some History

Many factors contribute to the lead that Europe and Asia have sustained in alliance activity. U.S. companies historically have enjoyed an enormous domestic market, and the very geography of the United States has provided diverse and scattered markets and also access to a broad range of natural resources. Those conditions have been reinforced by the markets and the resources of North American neighbors. Satisfied by large domestic markets, U.S. companies were not under particular pressure to form alliances until recently.

The European Background

Europe, by contrast, with its many, far smaller, countries, has always been a breeding ground of alliance activity. Over the centuries, the distinct national cultures were, of necessity, forced to look across their borders for allies, whether for military or economic sustenance. From the Hanseatic League that linked Baltic trading cities starting in the early thirteenth century to the *auld alliance* of France and Scotland to the European Union in the twentieth century, Europe's businesses have learned to do the same. For businesses in Scandinavia, Switzerland, the Netherlands, Belgium and Luxembourg, and more recently the Baltic nations, domestic economies simply did not offer the critical mass necessary for steady growth. Cross-border activity provided that opportunity.

At the same time, the political and economic fabric of Europe has woven government activity and ownership and also organized labor into corporate life to a far greater degree than is found in the United States. This has created restrictions on equity stakes and a stricter regulatory climate—conditions that have militated against mergers and acquisitions. Takeovers cannot be consummated unless business leaders, labor unions, and government officials deem them friendly. Under these circumstances, strategic alliances have gained momentum as the best way to access the capabilities of other companies, as well as the best ways of dealing with highly fragmented and heavily regulated markets.

In addition, fears have grown outside Europe of a *Fortress Europe,* reflecting the strength of the European Union, whose fifteen current nations hold 6.2 percent of the world's population and 20 percent of the world's gross domestic product (GDP). This view of Europe has led many companies outside the region to seek alliances with European companies, hoping to obtain market access. Some of these alliances are very successful, but many have failed because the overseas partner failed to understand either the local culture or the European partner's motivation for the alliance.

Europeans, for instance, have learned over the centuries to live with Realpolitik, hoping to avoid the devastation and economic disruption of their homelands that the continent's many wars formerly brought. In the business world the Realpolitik view translates into flexibility, at which most European companies excel. Contracts are negotiated and written with the idea that they may evolve as conditions change. In this environment, explicit understanding of a partner's goals and actions is essential to keep an alliance on track.

The Asian Background

In Asia, the major trading nations have not had the geographic proximity to as many neighbors as their counterparts in Europe, but other conditions have also led to a great deal of alliance activity. Over the decades, the keiretsu of Japan, and later the chaebols of South Korea, have created partnerships and alliances that are built around cross-equity arrangements (see Exhibit 6.2). Ties between manufacturers and suppliers are very tight, with research, product development, and cost improvement all matters for cooperation. Japanese management recognized the potential power of a keiretsu long ago and through such alliances enjoyed a powerful competitive advantage against go-it-alone rivals in the United States.

One condition that encouraged these alliances was the posture of the United States in the post–World War II years. Hoping to create a bulwark against the spread of communism in Asia, the United States encouraged the Japanese government to manage its economy and protect its home markets. The tight interplay of the government, large corporations, and trade associations provided a safe harbor in which alliances became a way of life. Japanese alliance momentum was also spurred by companies' relative freedom from the pressure of the financial markets, compared to U.S. companies. In Japan, and elsewhere in Asia, there has been little pressure to report quarterly earnings and to devise tactics and strategies that enhance short-term performance. This encouraged companies to take the long view and during alliance nego-

Exhibit 6.2.   Joint Ventures Predominate in Asia

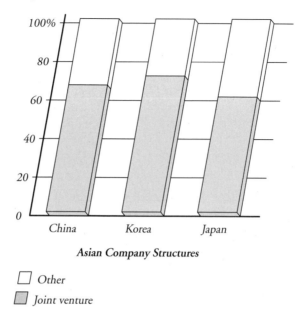

Asian Company Structures

☐ Other
▨ Joint venture

Source: Various national statistics; Booz·Allen & Hamilton estimates.

tiation to concentrate on operating rather than financial structure. And this latter posture positioned Japanese companies to obtain capabilities *from* their non-Japanese partners in preference to sharing capabilities *with* those partners. Over time the resulting operational excellence has strengthened the Japanese position considerably.

As a result of Japan's extraordinary success in building a trading economy, many other Asian nations are modeling their economies on Japan's. They too are embracing the central role of strategic alliances, working hard to develop their economies ever more quickly through such arrangements. What took 10 years in Japan at the outset of national development, China will do in 2.6 and South Korea in 3.3 years (see Exhibit 6.3).

Like European companies, Asian companies excel in their ability to be flexible. Contracts are written with the idea that they may change should conditions change. *Pardons* and *paroles* are accepted modes of behavior, and partners frequently ask for time-outs to reassess an alliance.

Exhibit 6.3.   A U.S. Lifetime Takes a Guangzhou Decade

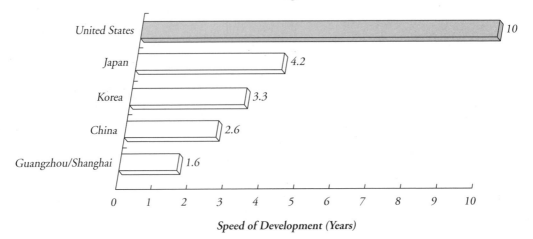

Speed of Development (Years)

How Americans Are Perceived by the Alliance Leaders

European and Asian executives find that their U.S. counterparts lag in the critical skills of planning integration and implementing. They are too quick to think the job is completed when the negotiations are finalized. Europeans and Asians now know that the negotiation stage is just the beginning (see Exhibit 6.4). These executives also believe that Americans have not institutionalized alliance knowledge and experience—and thus are not passing on lessons learned, spreading them throughout the organization.

These perceptions are all the more striking considering that generally Europeans and Asians have sought U.S. partners among companies experienced in alliances and thus are speaking about those experienced companies.

U.S. companies should take these views to heart. How prospective partners perceive them has major implications for the structure and ownership formulas of cross-border alliances. Of all the skill areas in which the Europeans and Asians have an edge, nowhere is the spread greater than in the negotiation and implementation stages. In all, there were twelve best practices in which the Europeans scored much higher

Exhibit 6.4.   U.S. Companies Are Rated Lower in Integration and Implementation

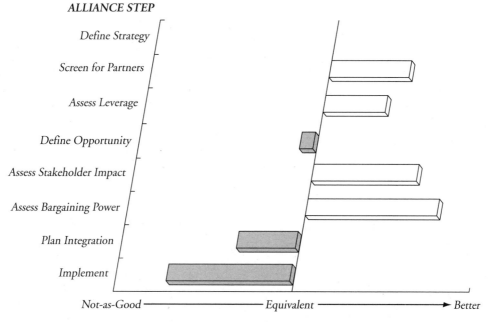

U.S. Skill Rated by Europeans and Asians

Source: Authors' surveys, 1994–1996.

than their U.S. counterparts, and the three largest spreads were in practices applying to negotiation and implementation:

In negotiation, the best practices were

- Assigning a negotiating team with alliance experience
- Coupling investment to performance
- Planning to build on the relationship

In implementation, the best practices were

- Planning for flexibility and change
- Designing the organizational structure to meet alliance needs
- Clearly defining management roles and empowerment
- Making lessons learned available in real time

Best practices that showed a smaller spread but were still significant were

- Determining the rationale of an alliance (versus going it alone)
- Assessing the alliance impact on the organization
- Preparing a realistic feasibility study
- Knowing the partner's alliance history
- Clearly defining the partner's capability gaps

Companies in the United States need to concentrate on these areas to become effective global partners in the age of collaboration.

Finally, we compared the overall concerns of U.S. and non-U.S. CEOs to see the relative attention paid to alliances. Among experienced cross-border alliance companies in Europe and Asia, the principal concerns of the CEOs were

- Managing multiple or global alliances
- Conveying to a partner the strategic intent of an alliance and the possibilities of expansion and further cooperation
- Anticipating and planning to meet the threats of other alliances
- Determining how much of the company's strategic intent to share with partners, stakeholders, and government officials

U.S. CEOs were more concerned with operational issues and also with negotiation, integration, and implementation. This lack of emphasis on strategic issues reflects Americans' relative lack of experience in cross-border alliances.

Arenas for Growth

As companies in the United States and other parts of the world steadily increase their alliance activity, a growing portion reach across borders. Doing business in a country other than one's own requires an understanding of cultural, political, and economic issues. For examples of what cross-border alliances can involve, we will look to the regions of Asia and Latin America.

Asia

Multinationals' interest and activity in Asian alliances has increased dramatically over the past few years, driven by the realization that in many industries Asia shows the greatest promise for growth, even considering the current setbacks in the "Asian crisis." In many cases, multinational corporations (MNCs) have also found alliances to be the necessary vehicle for market access.

The two critical challenges in Asian alliances, we have found, are the successful negotiation of the objectives and the initial implementation. Western companies focused on building or reinforcing their positions in Asia are faced with potential partners whose goals may be quite different. For Asian companies, these alliances often represent opportunities to supplement capabilities. Because the goals of the partners often vary greatly across the geographies, it is absolutely imperative for each company to understand the motivation and the cultural background from which the other company is operating.

Agreed-Upon Objectives When Partners Have Different Dreams. One key to agreeing on objectives with Asian partners is recognizing that their goals are driven in large part by the stage of economic development in their individual home countries and by their perceptions of Western countries' strengths and weaknesses. Here are some of the goals sought by companies in several Asian countries (also see Exhibit 6.5, which illustrates how local companies and MNCs in three Asian countries have different views of the two alliance goals of know-how and access).

China.   Beyond all other factors, Chinese companies are seeking technology know-how. They see technology as a design or a blueprint; they view its acquisition as a panacea, a quick way to catch up with the industrialized world. Often, however, when they acquire technology, they have a difficult time making it work. Although China has many engineers highly skilled at understanding product technology, these engineers have a more difficult time wrestling with process technology because it depends on mastering and embedding potentially imprecise operating philosophies rather than more precise technical specifications.

Exhibit 6.5.   Countries Have Evolving Goals

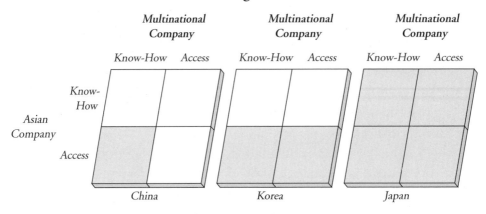

Local and MNC Goals by Asian Country

South Korea.   Western companies often find a similar emphasis on technology in South Korea but for different reasons. In many industry sectors, the chaebols have chosen not to be technology leaders, preferring to obtain the technology from elsewhere. They then use their highly refined process skills to produce the products more cheaply and more quickly—and in some cases provide better quality than rivals do. As a result they prefer alliances to take the form of technology licenses, which provide them a base technology on which they can later build. Samsung and Lucky Goldstar have been masters of this strategy and are viewed as models by other chaebols.

Japan.   Japanese firms generally believe that they have sufficient product and process technology. The challenges they face involve maintaining their competitiveness as they continue to expand their access and their global reach. Issues such as labor cost, local content restrictions, and currency fluctuations need to be dealt with—and have become increasingly complicated. Japanese firms have responded by placing greater emphasis on gaining access to global manufacturing and distribution networks. For many, alliances are the most practical and expedient way to gain network access.

India.   Many Indian companies are attractive alliance partners, not only for their knowledge of the local market and local conditions but for their strong distribution capabilities and quick market access. India also has a strong base in engineering skills, which has helped attract alliance partners such as Honda Motor and Acer, the Taiwanese computer maker. What the Indian companies are often looking for in alliance partners are financial muscle, opportunities to crack new markets abroad by tying into global brands, and knowledge gained from business experiences in other developing countries. Since the economy of the second most populous nation was liberalized in 1991, thousands of alliances have been formed between Indian companies and transnationals. Among the industries where alliances are most widespread are chemicals, electrical equipment, financial services, industrial machinery, food processing, telecommunications, and textiles. Recently the controls on the formation of alliances by public-sector companies have been eased, further spurring alliance activity.

Smooth Implementation: Pitfalls to Avoid.   The biggest pitfall we have observed in making alliances with Asian companies is that key success factors, and sometimes even the rationales for the alliances, are often lost during the negotiation process because of the urgency to consummate a deal. The emphasis on understanding partner motivations is important beyond the structuring of attractive terms that can prevail in the competition to form alliances because it is the understanding that can ensure that an alliance builds the appropriate capabilities and that the Western partner's interests are also met. Among the examples we have encountered in different places are these.

China.   The common lack of process capabilities in China means that the Western partner must ensure that such capabilities are built into the new entity. This is especially critical in the many cases where a joint venture is developed by absorbing an existing local operation. Building the process capabilities requires, among other things, an honest assessment of the number of expatriate production engineers and supervisors required and the duration of their stay, adequate training—overseas if necessary—for local engineers and production workers, and the phasing in of different stages of operations. At one client with whom we worked, the technology agreement specified that certain quality targets needed to be met before more sophisticated operations would be transferred to the new venture.

South Korea.   Given the ability of many South Korean companies to take a basic technology, duplicate it, and improve upon it, a critical issue for many Western firms is to maintain control over their technology. Western firms lax in this respect have found that they ended up contributing to the emergence of new competitors. Among the precautions often taken are limiting transfer of critical components, restricting local access to technical documentation, limiting transfer of design capability, and excluding source code from the technology transfer.

Japan.   The challenge in Japan is often to ensure that the venture agreement allows the Western firm access to the Japanese market. In more than one venture negotiation, the motivation of the Japanese partner was to create another worldwide node that would allow it to sell in the United States. Although this was a rational economic move, the U.S. partner had to ensure that it in turn received access to the Japanese market. In addition, plans to develop capabilities had to include the capabilities required for successful competition in the domestic Japanese market.

India.   Many Indian companies, after fulfilling their initial financial commitments to an alliance, have been unable to match the huge investments that their transnational partners have then decided to make. In some cases this has skewed alliance value, diluting the Indian company's equity and also its strategic value. In other cases the financial issue has thwarted and collapsed an alliance's bold plans. These possible outcomes make it essential to specify not just the initial financial commitment to the alliance but the anticipated financial needs as the alliance plays out. As elsewhere in Asia, careful partner selection and harmony in objectives are critical to creating a successful alliance. A sound alliance should allow room for partners' roles to change. Over time, partners must continually monitor the management of alliances, to keep abreast of one another's changing priorities.

Frictional Losses.   In addition to goal differences, beware *frictional losses,* another kind of pitfall that can endanger Western and Asian alliances. These frictional losses are often articulated by negotiators as communication problems with the potential partner: "Every point, even minor ones, seem to take forever to discuss because we have different frames of reference," or, "I would never have guessed that was the driver behind the problem—too bad it took so long to figure out."

These inefficiencies are rooted in different definitions and perceptions of competitiveness. In less-developed markets, like China, for example, the local partner may view personal relationships as a key to competitive success. Although that may be true in the near term, the success of most ventures depends more heavily on their having a rational economic structure. Indeed, it may even appear that a Chinese partner wants to do the deal for the deal's sake. Practically, forming a joint venture may mean instant pay raises for all local employees and substantial living benefits for the local managers. The Western partner needs to identify such issues quickly and find ways to address them without damaging the ultimate competitiveness of the alliance.

In our experience, many Western firms start by placing heavy emphasis on understanding and on bridging the local culture in order to reduce frictional loss. They then tend to undo their effort, however, by limiting expatriate terms of service, constantly rotating staff in and out of the venture. In some cases, such rotations make local employees unwilling to embrace new concepts. They resist the task of breaking down existing organizational barriers because they feel that the Western partner will not be around long enough to protect them against potential retaliation from their peers.

Success Factors for Doing Business in Asia!

The vision thing.   With 55 percent of the world's population, more than 20 percent of global GDP, Asia warrants corporate-level attention from Western alliance partners. Success requires a clearly articulated top-down vision for the region that is consistent with broader corporate objectives. This vision should establish clearly where the firm intends to go in the region, why, and what level of resources will be committed to getting there.

Look before you leap.   There is no "Asia Pacific." Asia is a portfolio of countries diverse in culture, size, stage of economic development—

and local "business system" and "style." Translating a global strategy into an Asian strategy therefore requires significant planning, research, analysis, and insight to prioritize where, when, and how to enter.

Be a farmer, not a hunter-gatherer.   One species of Chinese bamboo takes four years to sprout, then grows ninety feet in six months. So, too, with corporate growth. Building a sustainable position in most Asian markets requires a network of in-country relationships with the business and the government communities. These relationships take time to nurture but once in place can enable rapid growth.

Know-who versus know-how.   Relationships are strategic assets of the corporation. Decision processes, decision makers, and key decision influencers are not always apparent to outside observers. They need to be identified, cultivated, and managed as a critical resource and a source of competitive advantage.

Build a capability to manage alliances.   Influencing decision making on major projects or gaining access to otherwise closed components of a business system (distribution, for example) requires subtle relationship building at multiple levels. When this is beyond the ability even of empowered country managers, relationship gaps can be temporarily filled with a variety of well-managed alliances that build trust on many levels. Alliance management capabilities for using best practices—in the creation, maintenance, and dissolution of alliances—need to be planned for, and developed, in the region.

Promise only what you can deliver, and deliver what you promise. The small number of decision makers and influencers and the close links among them mean that both good news and bad news travels fast. Overpromising or underdelivering, anywhere in the country, or even the region, can adversely affect a firm's overall image and credibility.

Empower the people closest to the market.   Although the degree of coordination across the region needs to be carefully defined, as a general rule the complexity of each market and the importance of local relationships requires significant empowerment of the country manager within a preagreed strategic framework.

You never know who can play the violin until you ask.   Finding the right people is difficult, so cast a wide internal net. Often there are hidden pockets of expertise within a firm. A company old-timer, for instance, may have a past affiliation with the region, plus the benefits of maturity and an intrafirm "old boy" network.

A contract may be only the beginning of the negotiations.   Prepare for uncertainties and surprises. In such dynamic environments, there are often unexpected changes in the course of the negotiation or approval process. Do not always take a yes to mean yes; a memorandum of understanding should not be viewed as the beginning of closing the deal but as an invitation to start a long, interesting journey.

Enjoy the ride as well as the destination.   Inevitably, there will be frustrations along the way. Do not fight them. Asia is one of the most fascinating regions of the world. We all have a lot to learn from its deep and rich cultural heritage. Learn to savor the journey, as you move steadily toward realizing your vision.

Latin America

The economies of most Latin American countries are undergoing major change as they move away from the import-substitution economic model that has dominated the continent since the 1930s. Market-oriented policies have lowered the barriers to investment and trade and are drawing these countries ever closer to the global economy. Their role as competitive world suppliers of tradeables and the size of their growing markets are attracting new numbers of global firms. As trade barriers continue to fall, reinforced by the participation of the major countries in the regional common markets—Mercosur, the Andean Pact and Nafta—the prospects for continued growth are good (see Exhibit 6.6).

Companies with operations in Latin America are rushing to strengthen their existing positions in these dynamic markets, and new entrants from all over the globe are seeking to establish operations. Speed is of the essence as positions are staked out in the more attractive sectors. And this emphasis on speed as a competitive weapon, along with the traditional advantages of strategic alliances, helps explain the growth in the number of strategic alliances in Latin America.

Many global companies find it is faster to join forces with an established player than to start operations from scratch. They also find it is comforting to have a partner familiar with dealing with the continual

Exhibit 6.6.   Latin American Economies Are Undergoing Major Structural Changes

Historically
- *Strong government controls*
- *Unclear and changing "rules of the game"*
- *Foreign investment discrimination*

Today
- *More market driven economies*
- *Higher economic and political stability*
- *Foreign investment not viewed as a threat to political independence*

In the Future
- *Government policies more attuned with business drivers*
- *Lower trade barriers — greater exposure to global trends*
- *Greater integration with the global economy*

regulatory and legislative changes that have been a hallmark of the region in the past, particularly while the risk persists of a return to populist macroeconomic policies. As a result, multinationals and local companies have increasingly joined forces to respond to the opportunities and the challenges brought about by market opening and economic stabilization.

Typical Objectives: Know-How Versus Market Access.   After years of experience with captive and protected markets, local producers are suddenly having to deal with more efficient international competitors able to provide higher-quality goods and services at better prices. The impact on local industry has been profound: whole sectors are consolidating, and companies across the board are scrambling to improve efficiency and the quality of products and services. Local firms are seeking access to technology and capabilities that are critical for their survival in an environment of increased competition. The tradeable they offer prospective multinational partners is access to a large market with high growth prospects (see Exhibit 6.7 for the areas in which alliances are being forged in Latin America as compared to the rest of the world).

Exhibit 6.7.   Service Alliances Predominate in Latin America

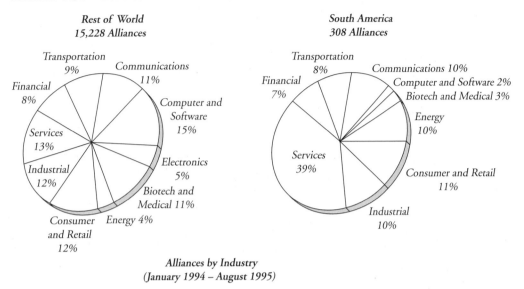

Rest of World
15,228 Alliances

Transportation 9%
Communications 11%
Financial 8%
Computer and Software 15%
Services 13%
Industrial 12%
Electronics 5%
Biotech and Medical 11%
Consumer and Retail 12%
Energy 4%

South America
308 Alliances

Transportation 8%
Communications 10%
Financial 7%
Computer and Software 2%
Biotech and Medical 3%
Energy 10%
Services 39%
Consumer and Retail 11%
Industrial 10%

Alliances by Industry
(January 1994 – August 1995)

Simultaneously, the increasing importance of the regional trade blocs is allowing successful firms across many industries to organize across national borders, raising the minimum scale needed to remain competitive. This has led many Latin American national companies to form cross-border alliances that expand their presence into neighboring countries and create regional players. The large capital requirements of some of the major new opportunities to build infrastructure are also contributing to alliance formation, particularly in such sectors as telecommunications and energy.

The vast majority of strategic alliances in Latin America fall into one of three categories, each involving a mixture of know-how and market access:

- Multinationals supplying technology and know-how to local firms in exchange for market access
- Leading multinationals or regional firms joining together—often across borders—in regional ventures to increase the scale of their operations
- Large providers of capital joining forces with industry specialists to take advantage of major infrastructure opportunities

Family Firms and a History of Macroeconomic Instability.   As elsewhere, building successful alliances in Latin America requires an understanding of the business culture and practices on the continent and in the various countries, although Latin American countries are more similar to each other than are Asian or European countries. At least for the most important economies, differences relate more to relative size (Brazil's dominant position in the Mercosur, the Colombia-Venezuela axis in the Andean Pact) than to fundamental differences in the stage of their economic development. In fact, most Latin American countries share four critical elements that to one extent or another have shaped their business environment.

High inflation.   With the notable exceptions of Colombia and Chile, many Latin American countries have a relatively recent history of endemic high inflation. This inflation led many companies to focus on the short term, with long-term planning and market understanding relegated to secondary considerations. This makes it particularly critical to build vision and active strategy management into any new venture. Positions based on sustainable competitive advantage rather than superior financial flexibility require the disciplined application of market-oriented delivery skills—and these need to be built into the alliance. Because such skills are often in short supply, the partners need to agree explicitly on how to provide for them in the context of the alliance.

Closed economies.   The short-term orientation engendered by high inflation has been complemented by a relative unconcern for marketing issues and understanding because so many markets were protected. In spite of improvements in recent years, most approaches to market intelligence remain relatively unsophisticated, and market knowledge is often informal and difficult to access. It is thus critical for the partners to ensure that a formal market analysis capability is built into the alliance so it can systematically develop a thorough information base.

Government intervention.   For many years, success in Latin America depended as much on an ability to cope with repeated and often abrupt government intervention, in the form of regulatory and tax changes, as it did on market responsiveness or cost competitiveness. Return on investment will to some extent continue to depend on each country's overall growth as much as on the performance of the individual firm. Yet the balance of elements necessary for success is weighted ever more heavily toward free market factors. Although it is still important to be able to react quickly to policy shifts, any alliance needs a clear plan for achieving cost competitiveness.

Family-owned businesses.   Many important businesses in Latin America are run by families. This has three important consequences for alliance formation, each of which is a sensitive issue, underlining the importance of diplomacy in discussions:

- Businesses are often not accustomed to the level of information disclosure that is common in countries with more developed capital markets.
- Businesses' ownership and management power structures often overlap in ways that are not always immediately transparent.
- Linked to this ownership-management overlap, businesses often show visible reluctance to give up control to an alliance.

A company from outside the region must take these elements into account in order to understand the local partner's agenda and to define the alliance objectives. These elements can create additional complexities, and they certainly reinforce the need for a focus on the strategic objectives and an agreement on how the alliance should be managed. In negotiating with a family-owned potential partner, for example, the first hurdle is to obtain sufficient accurate information for an alliance to be structured. Then potential differences about the management of the venture need to be bridged. This is likely to require more negotiating than in alliances that do not involve cross-cultural partners. Ensuring professional management of the alliance is not always easy. The clear discussion of objectives becomes crucial, so as to provide objective orientation guidelines for alliance management action.

Yet clear, agreed-upon alliance objectives are not sufficient by themselves. In some cases the ownership-management overlap has meant that the negotiator did not have sufficient mandate: deals have been dissolved after an agreement had apparently been reached because an important shareholder exercised veto power unexpectedly. In dealing with private and family-owned firms, it pays to do your homework on the power structure of the prospective partner.

The importance of the control issue makes assessment of the alliance-acquisition trade-off particularly important, both during initial alliance-structuring negotiations and in contingency planning. An alliance is often seen in Latin America as a first step toward a later acquisition by the stronger partner. This perception may cause pressures for an early outright sale rather than an alliance. It certainly means partners must understand possible future control and ownership outcomes at the time they are structuring the alliance.

The possibility that a country might return to the economic instability of the past reinforces the importance of establishing contingency plans for terminating the alliance. The exit clause takes on additional significance as a country risk-management tool. The combination of the relative importance of control concerns and of macroeconomic uncertainty makes exit clauses in Latin American alliances an even more crucial part of the equation than they are in alliances elsewhere.

Seven Success Factors for Alliances in Latin America!

Understand the terrain.   The fiscal and regulatory conditions in many countries are complex. Brazil, for example, has nearly seventy different taxes, the imposition basis of which can significantly influence the structure of an alliance. Not only are these conditions complex but they change regularly. Despite substantially greater predictability in recent years, fiscal developments need to be monitored closely. An unexpected change in regulations or tax rules, if it catches an alliance off-guard, can be expensive.

Do not decline invitations for coffee.   Establishing relationships with the government and business community is critical. Such networks are information sources about trends in the economy overall and in the conditions and business opportunities in the alliance's sphere of interest. It is more natural in Latin America than in most other parts of the world that these relationships extend beyond pure business discussions to the personal dimension. This helps build trust.

Learn how to spot coded messages.   Potential partners will not always be up front with what they want and what they think. They may hint at a situation or talk in general terms and expect to be understood. As the Brazilian saying goes: "For a good listener, half a word is sufficient."

Promise only what you can deliver, and deliver what you promise.   As in Asia, the number of important decision makers is relatively small, and they are invariably connected through multiple personal and business ties. This means that reputations spread very fast, and credibility is important. Credibility can be achieved only by exercising disciplined consistency both in communication content and in actions with potential alliance partners.

Look for bicultural people.   The explosive growth in alliances in recent years means that well-trained people are scarce. Those particularly effective in an alliance will understand the international background of the many know-how providers as well as the local culture and business practices of the market where the alliance operates. The facilitation skills that such people provide are often crucial to realizing the full potential of an alliance.

A word is just a word.   Expect uncertainties, surprises, and unexpected changes. A presumed final commitment might turn out to be just another negotiation step. Approval processes may have hidden dimensions, especially in family-owned business. Even after the alliance is formed, renegotiation and further bargaining may be sought, with changes in the environment cited as justification. This makes it particularly important to think through the possible implications of an agreement in a wide range of different scenarios.

The control thing.   Many Latin American firms have clear groups who exercise broad control, and many are managed as family businesses even when there are significant minority shareholders. Many business leaders see the control of alliances as their natural prerogative. Facing the question of control up front and creating a professional management structure is critical for the success of any alliance.

The Wake-Up Call

Only in the 1980s, as Japanese and European alliances vigorously entered the domestic U.S. markets, did many U.S. companies hear the wake-up call. With long trust-based relationships and alliance experience,

Japanese and European competitors enjoyed huge advantages in economies of scale, an ability to cross borders to exploit different national markets, and a well-established control of the supply chain. They also learned product quality techniques and gained know-how in cutting the cycle time and experience in financial exchange management. Among the U.S. industries that reeled under this competition were auto manufacturing, shipbuilding, consumer electronics, photocopiers, steel, and home appliances.

To meet the challenge from overseas, managers in the United States finally turned to the alliance approach, in the same way that the Europeans and Asians had turned to alliances in the 1960s to respond to the challenge from large U.S. manufacturers. Now companies everywhere, even those once slow to form global alliances, are embracing the alliance option to increase their competitive strength and to stimulate growth and profits.

Chapter 7

Legal and Governance Perspectives on Strategic Alliances

In preceding chapters we have discussed the whys, hows, whens, and whats of strategic alliances. But bear in mind that every strategic alliance is not just a business undertaking but also an exercise in business law, made all the more complicated by increasing globalization and the blurring of industry lines.

As corporations and their managers conduct their surveillance of the competitive environment, screen and analyze potential partners, and consider opportunities, many legal issues, both large and small, must be addressed. To take but one example, James G. Archer, a partner with Sidley & Austin, a New York law firm with a large practice in strategic alliances, notes that "in Spain, all directors are required by law to attend the annual stockholders' meeting. At directors' meetings, directors may vote by proxy. But at stockholders' meetings, they must appear."

Experienced alliance managers have learned that seeking advice from legal, accounting, and tax experts early in the process helps build a strong alliance foundation. It is essential that they find experts who have significant experiences in alliance formation and governance. Many complex legal, regulatory, and environmental concerns are best analyzed well in advance, so that alliance partners may begin the often overlong process toward approval even as they negotiate their deal.

We recommend an overall alliance structure based on the principles of what we call the *governance pyramid,* illustrated in Exhibit 7.1. Built correctly, this governance structure will stand the test of time. If not, it can come tumbling down.

In the early days of the alliance formation process, managers should consult with their legal experts for instruction and briefing on what issues to address during the negotiations. Later the lawyers can help managers ensure that each partner understands what the other expects and that the agreements spell out clearly what the partners intend. They can examine and explain the tax codes in the area where the alliance's activities will be based and the impact those laws will have on partners' taxes. They can assist managers in understanding what steps they must take to protect investors and respect workers' rights. In many European countries, for example, companies are required to have a *supervisory board* that

Exhibit 7.1.   Governance Is the Most Overlooked Element

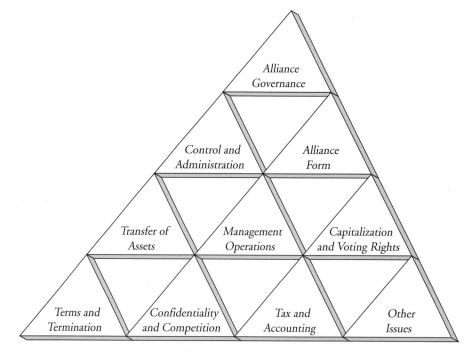

Governance Pyramid

includes a labor representative. In some cases this board has consultative powers; in others it may have veto powers. Entering into an alliance without planning how to address these conditions is self-defeating.

Preparing for Worst-Case Scenarios

Nowhere is the need for legal understanding more manifest than in worst-case scenarios: when an alliance is deadlocked over how to proceed or when it slips toward dissolution. Having clear procedures for breaking deadlocks and also for divorce proceedings can ensure that the requirements of all parties are achieved and parties' interests protected.

Sidley & Austin has spelled out seven methods that might be used to break a deadlock. To be of service when a crisis unfolds, each of these must be put in place when the alliance is first formed:

1. Establish a board of directors for the alliance with *an odd number of directors*. How this board will be filled and with whom is, of course, a delicate matter for negotiation.
2. Assign to the chair or chief executive of the alliance *the right to cast a tie-breaking vote* when directors reach a deadlock. Note, however, that in some countries, corporate law does not permit such a step.
3. Create a mechanism through which *deadlocked issues are passed directly to the CEOs of the parent companies.* This can work in two ways, Archer has said, by providing a "big picture" review of the sticking points and by encouraging settlement to avoid the embarrassment of having to ask the corporate parents to solve the alliance's mess.
4. Permit one partner to *put in more than its share* as a loan or dilutive equity contribution if the disagreement is over whether to invest additional funds from the parents. This can prevent a budget impasse that would block alliance growth.
5. Negotiate a provision for *a forced buyout*. Remember the tried-and-true method when two children argue over how to share a dessert? One child makes the cut, and the other gets to choose a piece first. Sidley & Austin often recommends that alliances include a provision under which one partner can name a price at which it will buy out

or sell to the other and the other partner then chooses whether to buy or sell. A major difficulty with this mechanism comes when the two partners have different bargaining power. Nonetheless, Archer says, this provision provides a rational means of breaking a deadlock—and it is a natural restraint that encourages the partners to find ways to make the alliance work.

6. Include a provision that gives either partner *the right to compel dissolution* of the alliance. In most cases where this right is exercised, the alliance's assets are auctioned to the highest bidder, whether one of the partners or an outside party. The negative effect of this provision is that it gives the dissatisfied partner the power to give up. It is thus a disincentive for exploring other alternatives.

7. Negotiate a provision that grants one alliance partner *the right to break deadlocks* over the future of the alliance. Coming to agreement on such a provision is clearly one element in delicate negotiations.

However elaborate the mechanisms for breaking a deadlock, they still may not be enough. Some alliances invariably fail, to the disappointment of both partners. Among the more prominent causes of alliance failure are these:

• One partner breaches the terms of the alliance agreement. An alliance agreement should specify clearly what actions and conditions constitute a breach. One alternative to dissolving the alliance after a breach is to shift greater control to the partner that did not default. This may be less disruptive and harmful to both partners than terminating the alliance.

• A government takes an adverse action. Such actions include expropriation of venture assets, changes in tax laws, imposition of currency controls, lack of protection for technology or intellectual assets such as patents or copyrights, and interference with the exercise of voting rights.

• The partners fail to obtain necessary government approvals. The European Union, for example, has rigorous competition laws that are often difficult to interpret as an alliance is being negotiated. Alliance partners have found, to their dismay, that the notification, clearance, and exemption process can take considerable time, even years. And partners may find that a negotiated deal has to be modified to suit the findings of the European Commission.

- One of the parent companies is acquired. The remaining original partner might be gravely concerned if it then finds itself in an alliance with a bitter rival. However, an alliance agreement that prohibits either partner from accepting a takeover offer is unlikely to be enforceable. More feasible options might be to provide an option for the acquiring company to buy out or sell to the remaining original partner (sometimes that sale can be at a bargain price) or for such a change in ownership to trigger a shift in control of the alliance's board to the remaining original partner.
- One partner files for bankruptcy protection.
- The partners agree that the alliance has failed to meet their goals.
- The agreement expires after the number of years specified at signing.

If there is to be any hope that a divorce can proceed smoothly, numerous details must be negotiated at the time the alliance is formed. These include how the alliance's assets will be valued and appraised, how the assets will be distributed, who will be permitted to use technology developed by the alliance and under what restrictions, how the proceeds of any sale will be distributed among the partners, whether licenses transferred by the parents to the alliance will revert to the parents or be available to each partner, and how to deal with unfunded liabilities and pension obligations.

Specifying Structure, Control, and Funding

In the early days of prospecting for alliances, as partners are screened and opportunities evaluated, an awareness of legal issues and concerns can provide the broad framework that should underlie the business and financial analyses. Perhaps the most basic of issues is what legal structure the alliance will take: will it be a corporation in which the parent companies transfer assets to the new concern in exchange for stock, or will it be a partnership or limited liability corporation?

Other major issues on which Sidley & Austin advises clients to focus are the management and control of the alliance, whether interests in the alliance may be transferred to other parties, what resources will be provided by each partner, and how profits (or losses) will be allocated. Reciprocity is usually the rule. "Whatever protection your client gets," cautions Archer, "it will likely have to give." A would-be partner must decide whether it assigns higher priority to gaining flexibility (which its partner will also gain) or to placing restrictions on its partner (and accepting restrictions itself).

Many alliances lay a weak foundation for the future when they overspecify in the contract what they expect of each other. By spelling out in detail all manner of required conduct, the partners wind up losing the flexibility the alliance will need to respond nimbly to changes in the environment. Nonetheless, some basics must be negotiated carefully:

- What is the most efficient legal structure for the alliance in terms of taxes and liabilities?
- What is the scope of the alliance? This answer to this question must carefully delineate permissible areas of competition between the alliance and its parents.
- What cash, services, and property will each partner commit to the alliance? What happens if more is needed than originally planned?
- What economic rewards and penalties should be built in to encourage interdependency?
- How should major risk contingencies be addressed, such as a change in the regulatory climate that changes how business is done in a particular market?

In many cases alliance agreements make provision for the raising of additional funds, be they from outside lenders or from the shareholders or partners. Generally, the directors of the parent companies have the right of approval over such funding requests. Gregg Kirchhoefer, a partner in the Chicago office of Kirkland & Ellis, another law firm active in alliances, recommends that alliance partners specify in their initial agreement a financial test of whether additional funding is needed, either debt-to-equity ratio or some objective performance milestone.

Alliance partners also need to agree on the use of generally accepted accounting principles, taking particular care to reconcile differing national rules.

Heeding Regulatory Issues

Kirchhoefer also recommends that would-be partners conduct a rigorous antitrust analysis before signing an alliance agreement. When General Motors and Toyota agreed in 1983 to the joint venture known as NUMMI, they faced extensive antitrust scrutiny from the U.S. Department of Justice and had to modify their initial agreement before winning permission to proceed. Similarly, the sweeping alliance announced in 1996 between British Airways and American Airlines faced protracted review and modification before European regulators were satisfied. "The parties should avoid any collusion outside the strategic alliances' legitimate activities and should analyze additional antitrust risks which may arise in the future operation of the strategic alliance," Kirchhoefer cautions.

Anticipating another regulatory hurdle, he also recommends that alliance partners closely review past activities at all facilities and sites that the alliance will operate to determine whether they face any environmental liabilities. A due diligence review should generally include an environmental audit of each property by a qualified consultant. And because such audits can take a long while to complete, Kirchhoefer recommends that they be undertaken well in advance of the finalization of the alliance.

As competition races across borders, more laws and more nations come into play. It is essential, of course, to evaluate closely how corporate formalities and laws differ by country. Many countries provide *worker participation rights,* for example, that are vastly different from U.S. law. "Read an English translation of the laws—and their legislative history—as well as talking to a qualified local lawyer," Archer advises U.S. companies. "But, remember, there are likely to be differences between an American lawyer's interpretation of translated words and the concept in foreign law."

Local investment laws deserve particular scrutiny. In contemplating alliances, would-be partners must consider whether local laws restrict the percentage of foreign ownership or mandate a specific level of local ownership. They must ask, too, whether local law requires government approval of initial or subsequent investments, withdrawal of funds, or conversion of payments into other currencies. Finally, protection of the parents' and the alliance's intellectual property may be unsatisfactory. "Be aware that foreign laws may not be based solely on promoting competition," advises Archer. "They may have a basis in policies that provide significant protection for local interests."

In cases where government approval—international, national, provincial, state, or municipal—is required, the alliance agreement should assign responsibility for obtaining those approvals to one of the partners, and the agreement should be contingent upon receipt of those approvals. Bear in mind, too, that alliance governance incorporated into a corporate charter or bylaw is likely to be more readily enforced in many countries than are contractual provisions between the parent companies.

In parts of the developing world and the emerging democracies, an essential issue is how well established and trustworthy the legal system itself is. Alliance partners may want to examine whether their investments can be secured with real or intangible assets outside the foreign country or whether political risk insurance is a reasonable precaution.

On the tax front it is hard to generalize, given the multiplicity of tax laws, tax codes, and tax considerations, particularly on a global basis. In alliances as in all business matters, tax experts agree, the tax tail should never wag the business dog. Yet some basic tax considerations underlie most alliance strategy. Albert S. Golbert, a partner in Golbert Kimball & Weiner of Los Angeles, summarized them in a presentation to the Los Angeles County Bar Association:

- Reduce the global tax rate to, at the very least, a rate no higher than the home country's tax rate.
- Provide sufficient foreign-source income in the appropriate "baskets" to take advantage of available foreign tax credits.
- Balance borrowings so that interest deductions are not disallowed.
- Avoid tax authority reallocation of income, either through deemed distributions or transfer-pricing initiatives.

Going Beyond Legalities to Cooperation

Finally, who sits at the negotiating table is just as important as what is discussed there. "The best scenario for a company involves creating a team with managers who will work for the alliance and have its best interests at heart and also managers who will not participate in the alliance and have only the parent company's interest at heart," Archer says. Legal representatives can certainly do double-duty as watchdogs—but they are no substitute for having the managers most directly affected at the table.

Ultimately, the real benefits of a strategic alliance are never realized simply through careful, detailed contracts defining the partners' obligations. "Making an alliance work requires a cooperative attitude and a successful business relationship," Archer concludes. "Rigidly defined obligations are not enough."

Chapter 8

Institutionalizing Alliance Capabilities

The Secrets of Repeatable Success

As the previous chapters have shown, alliances are surging in popularity, and they are yielding superior returns on investment. In addition, the more experience a company gains in creating alliances, the greater its returns from them. We are convinced that alliances are a central, essential, and permanent engine for driving corporate growth and profitability. In this age of collaboration, only through allying can companies obtain the capabilities and resources necessary to win in the changing global marketplace. Self-reliance is an option few companies are still able to afford.

Many companies are being thrust into situations where they will need to form multiple alliances. These companies recognize the distinct advantages alliances can yield. They are also conscious of the limited resources they have for developing differential capabilities to fill their skills and knowledge gaps, as their industry boundaries blur and they cope with global expansion and technological change.

Some corporate leaders are going beyond conducting a series of individual alliance building efforts and are creating an institutional alliance capability. Americans are newer to this game than Europeans and Asians, as they are still improving their skills in the best practices, still learning how to form an alliance and make it work. However, it is an important step because the companies that take a rigorous and disciplined approach to building an institutional alliance capability have significantly higher returns on their alliances than do other companies (see Exhibit 8.1).

The capability for building alliances evolves in companies and so does the institutionalizing of the alliance capability. This chapter traces those evolutionary courses, illustrating multiple ways in which companies are making the skills of alliance building a permanent part of their organizations.

Rationale for Institutionalizing

We all struggle with learning in life. Most of our learning is experience based, and in most cases we accumulate it as individuals. As adolescents, we did not have much interest in learning from our elders. Now, as

Exhibit 8.1.   Companies with High Returns on Alliances Are More Disciplined in Following a Process

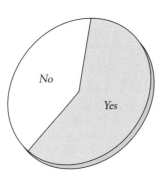

Alliance Process Used?

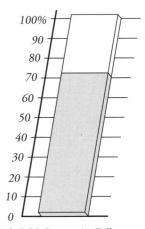

High-ROI Companies Follow Disciplined Alliance Process

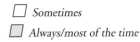

☐ *Sometimes*

▨ *Always/most of the time*

Source: Booz·Allen & Hamilton survey on institutionalizing alliance capabilities, 1997.

managers in corporations, many of us act similarly, continuing to insist on learning from our own mistakes. The research of the authors of this book shows that this has certainly been true for most companies engaged in making alliances, where learning by doing has been the traditional way. Practical-minded executives justify this by asserting there is no substitute for learning by doing. Up to a point they are right, but the alliance stakes are becoming too important to be left to the vicissitudes of unschooled management.

Some alliance-building companies, for example, average an 87 percent success rate on their alliances (according to their own standards for success, as described in Chapter Five), whereas others average only 37 percent (see Exhibit 8.2). Strikingly, the more successful alliance companies may have figured out how to do alliances, but they have been unable to achieve similarly successful results with acquisitions. Both groups of companies had an achievement ratio of only about 50–50 on acquisitions. However, these successful alliance companies also enjoy

Exhibit 8.2.   Some Companies Average an 87 Percent Success Rate (but Fare Worse in Acquisitions)

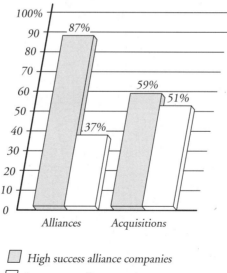

Source: Booz·Allen & Hamilton survey on institutionalizing alliance capabilities, 1997.

higher profitability on their alliances—20 percent versus only 11 percent for the less successful companies (see Exhibit 8.3). This 1997 survey differential is consistent with results from our earlier surveys.

Success in alliances also translates into superior growth. On average, the successful companies see alliances contributing more to current revenues, and more important, the alliance capability positions them for faster growth over the next five years. As mentioned earlier, the successful companies expect about 35 percent of their future revenues to come from alliances, up steeply from the current 21 percent (see Exhibit 8.4).

These successful companies are also more than twice as likely to be engaged in a strategic alliance as in a more modest transactional one. It is easy to see the linkage between the strategic nature of most of their alliances and the higher growth they anticipate.

Although more than 60 percent of CEOs in the United States approve of alliances, approaching the acceptance rate in Europe and Asia

Exhibit 8.3.   Successful Alliance Companies Earn More Profits on Their Alliances

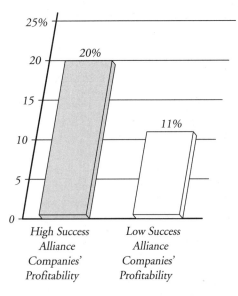

Source: Booz·Allen & Hamilton survey on institutionalizing alliance capabilities, 1997.

Exhibit 8.4.   Successful Alliance Companies Depend More on Alliances for Growth

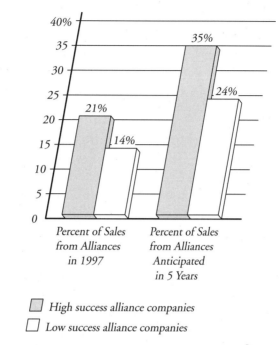

Source: Booz·Allen & Hamilton survey on institutionalizing alliance capabilities, 1997.

(see Exhibit 0.1), when CEOs and executives are newcomers to the world of multiple alliances, they find managing the arrangements the most frustrating element. Armed with an understanding of the rewards and motivations for institutionalizing an alliance capability process, companies find it easier simply to plunge ahead.

Choosing the Right Approach: Some Roads to Nowhere

Battle-tested alliance executives are often suspicious, and rightly so, of bureaucratic management processes. Some executives maintain that ad hoc management and pure luck play an important role in success. Luck certainly helps any alliance reach its goals. We believe, however, that the "luckiest" and most successful companies are those that learn from others. As baseball executive Branch Rickey once said, "Luck is the residue of design."

In our examination of scores of failed and failing approaches to institutionalizing alliance capability, we have identified a number of overly limited approaches, which companies will want to consciously surpass, and even some roads to nowhere, which companies will want to avoid.

The Ad Hoc Approach: Rising to the Occasion Each Time

Most companies evolve their alliance approach and capability over time. Taking the ad hoc approach is how most companies in the United States behave today. In a company taking this approach, little knowledge is captured and few best practices. People are essentially on their own, learning how to do alliances based on their individual experiences. In an environment with few alliances, this is adequate. But considering the increasing importance of alliances, before too long this approach is likely to produce frustrating and unsatisfactory results for the company.

Most organizations are culturally resistant to change. Starting a strategic alliance process without recognizing this, and without an approach to overcoming it, is like playing Russian roulette. Most U.S. auto manufacturers, for example, chose the ad hoc approach in answering the Japanese assault on their home market. Ford, however, took a step back and marshaled its strengths and resources in a focused manner to negotiate a historic alliance with Mazda. Today Ford and Mazda are so intertwined that it is sometimes difficult to know where one starts and the other finishes. Ford and Mazda are building and institutionalizing alliance capability to extend their joint reach across the globe.

The Lone Ranger and Tonto Approach: Relying on Specialists

In some companies the alliance learning of the corporation resides in one or two specialists who are called in during negotiations to act as the gunslingers of alliance knowledge. This is often quite helpful but has two drawbacks. First, as the number of alliances surges, the Lone Ranger and Tonto are quickly overtaxed, even if they have a small group of deputies. Second, the specialists, given the demands on them, are usually involved only in the formation of the alliance and not in its management or the institutionalization of alliance skills.

That arrangement leaves the operating entities and managers without the guidance and assistance they need. Sometimes *action fever* grows so swiftly that it threatens to sweep away good strategic sense. Such fevers often stem from senior managers' enthusiasm and ad hoc, antibureaucratic thinking. But without clear commitment to best practice development, training, monitoring, rigorous analysis, and open communication, many strategic alliance processes actually breed tension, frustrations, and suspicion. Such outcomes create unbridgeable gaps. It is not surprising that executives who are hired in the Lone Ranger role become frustrated and often leave the company within five years, taking their knowledge and experience with them.

The Ivory Tower Syndrome:
Creating a Citadel of Alliance Thinkers

Some companies view alliance management as an academic art that can be mastered only by specialists steeped in theories, grids, and frameworks. We have seen outsiders (consultants) and corporate staff specialists hired to work in splendid isolation, divorced from the realities of the corporate strategic direction and operational requirements. In these situations the chief alliance executive has very little impact on development of the strategy behind the alliance and usually plays the role of critical reviewer or sounding board for senior management's alliance ideas.

One of our clients recognized that its strategic alliance process was exhibiting ivory tower syndrome, paying more attention to the review process than to increasing business value and to filling gaps in corporate and strategic business unit strategy and capability. Operating managers had learned how to submit plans that would satisfy the elaborate alliance review process so the managers could get on with their businesses. In response to this situation, the CEO restructured the alliance structure. Corporate alliance reviews, once a ritual process, were now held at variable intervals that reflected the pace of change in the underlying industry and the significance of the issues confronting alliance formation and management.

The Not-Invented-Here Complex: Failing to Keep an Open Mind

Failing to learn from others generally produces disastrous consequences. Strategic alliance management and processes often stagnate. The successful companies see alliances as a rifle rather than an automatic weapon. They make periodic and thoughtful assessments of their capabilities and priorities. They use alliances to fill key capability gaps where acquisitions and in-house development are not appropriate approaches. They also understand their company culture and how it influences behavior, both inside their organization and outside.

Such companies recognize the importance of alliances to their success and reach out for knowledge and expertise to create a well-oiled alliance capability. They know from experience that learning counts—and counts big. They set up systems and processes to transfer alliance learning and experience to key managers. They also create repositories of knowledge for managers to tap into. They know that to manage multiple alliance arrangements takes more than in-house efforts. It is not surprising to find that the most forward-looking alliance-building companies—including Oracle, Xerox, IBM, Hewlett-Packard, Motorola, Merck, and Johnson & Johnson—have each formed well over one hundred alliances.

The One-Flavor-Fits-All Approach: Failing to Select the Right Management Structure and Managers

There are no one-flavor-fits-all management structures, although some companies act as though there are. The alliance management structure needs to be tailored for each company, because the critical issues, challenges, and degrees of freedom differ significantly from one opportunity to the next. Xerox, for example, chose the corporate route, creating a corporate group to be relationship managers for key alliances such as Fuji Xerox. The job of the relationship manager is to coordinate across the alliance partners. This system offers many advantages and some unique challenges. Many issues need to be examined before choosing a management structure—impact on value creation, implementation power, conflict with other functions, and leverage across strategic business units (SBUs).

Similarly, there are no one-flavor-fits-all managers, and having the ability to select the right kind of alliance managers is critical. When an alliance objective is to create a new market, for example, the alliance's operating manager should exhibit entrepreneurial characteristics—being a change handler, having confidence, and being able to judge risks are crucial abilities. Choosing someone who is an evaluator, control oriented and measurement driven, is a formula for failure in a growing business. Yet we see many companies that do not match the individual to the strategy. Relying on an alliance management structure that does not yield the flexibility to deal with strategic issues places the alliance option in peril before it can achieve anything.

Such roads to nowhere will not lead companies to management systems and processes where strategic priorities can be translated into actions. The most successful alliance builders have developed a disciplined approach and rigorous methodology.

Institutionalizing an Alliance Capability: The Building Blocks of Success

The most successful companies have evolved their approaches to and capabilities for successful multiple-alliance management over time (Exhibit 8.5). They begin with the ad hoc approach just described, and we have noted that most companies in the United States are now at this level, with little knowledge capture and few best practices. Then they evolve to the Lone Ranger approach. And finally they move to the most skilled level, the institutional approach. Here, procedures are normalized, often with a dedicated staff engaged in a high degree of sharing. A repository of knowledge is established for future use. There are many variations in the ways companies have sought to build such an institutional alliance capability, and no one "right" approach. Lotus Development Corp., acquired by IBM in 1995, provides one good example of how the institutionalization of alliance skills might be addressed.

Exhibit 8.5.   Most Firms Evolve Their Alliance Capability

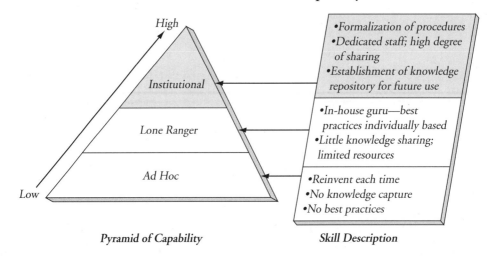

| Pyramid of Capability | Skill Description |

In the early 1980s, Lotus was floundering generally and had no disciplined approach to its alliances. Recognizing the importance of strategic alliances to its overall success, however, it decided in 1992 to build an alliance organization, which quickly grew to about fifty people. Underscoring the importance of alliances, the business development function reported to the alliance organization's vice president—an unusual reversal of the relationship at many companies. Lotus also assigns relationship managers to each alliance, and they are involved not only in the formation of the alliance but also in its implementation and management. When IBM completed its acquisition of Lotus, it left the alliance management structure largely unchanged.

The following activities provide a strong foundation for a successful institutionalized alliance capability process.

Capturing Best Practices

Knowing that alliance profitability improves as a company gains alliance experience (recall that experienced firms earn twice the return on investment from their alliances as inexperienced firms) has inspired many companies to try to jump-start the alliance learning curve by developing a set of best practices (see Exhibit 8.6). More than 90 percent of the com-

Exhibit 8.6.   Many Companies Are Moving to Capture Alliance Best Practices

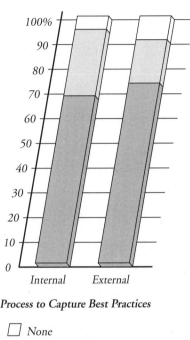

Process to Capture Best Practices

☐ None

▨ One-time

▨ Periodically

Source: Booz·Allen & Hamilton survey on institutionalizing alliance capabilities, 1997.

panies we surveyed recently have a process in place to capture best practices. Moreover, about 60 percent of them attempt to periodically capture internal best practices; about 70 percent attempt to periodically capture external best practices in alliances.

This is a remarkable improvement over where companies were five years ago, but it begs a question. If so many companies are capturing best practices, why aren't the success rates even higher? We suggest answers to that question in the remainder of this chapter.

Hewlett-Packard is one company that recognized early the importance of best practice capture to its alliance success. HP had always recognized that alliances were an important element of its value creation strategy. Through the late 1980s and early 1990s, it formed scores of alliances, and senior management assumed that managers were getting up to speed by attending seminars taught by academics and business schools. At the corporate level, no one was really thinking about technology leakage, exit mechanisms, governance issues, equity commitments, or other key alliance issues.

This all changed in the early nineties when, to the shock of corporate executives who thought everything was fine, HP surveyed its managers and found an overwhelming number of them ranked "strategic alliances" as the main area where they wanted more training. The external seminars the managers were attending, they said, were interesting, but they were not HP specific, and there were no best practices or particular techniques to follow.

Responding to the survey, Hewlett-Packard took some specific and dramatic steps. Today HP's best practice development is both internally and externally driven. Internally, an in-house best practice program develops and maintains training sessions, case histories, tool kits, and checklists. This material is then reinforced with assessments by alliance partners, comparisons with external best practices of other successful companies, and outside case studies. In short, HP has adopted a disciplined approach to best practice development that it now sees as a significant advantage it has over competitors (see Exhibit 8.7).

Employing Process Discipline

Two-thirds of the executives responding to our survey in the spring of 1997 reported that they have an alliance process. Strikingly, though, almost a third of the executives said they do *not* follow that process. Seems like fodder for the *Dilbert* comic strip, where Dilbert's company places too much emphasis on creating processes and not enough on making sure they are used and that they lead to improvements! At the same time, the survey clearly established that successful companies are more disciplined in following an alliance process than unsuccessful companies. The successful companies do better at planning integration, assessing bargaining power, and assessing leverage (see Exhibit 8.8). These are also the areas where the high success companies are more likely than

Exhibit 8.7. HP Recognizes the Importance of Capturing Alliance Best Practices

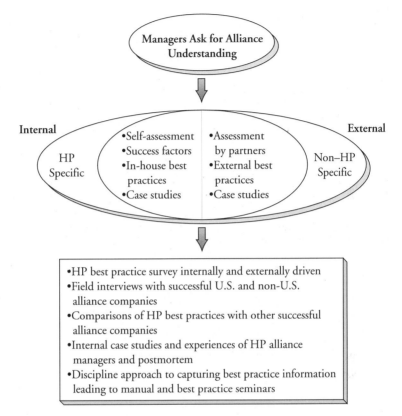

Source: Booz·Allen & Hamilton survey on institutionalizing alliance capabilities, 1997.

the low success companies to incorporate the alliance methodology in their process.

Similarly almost everyone incorporates some aspect of defining strategy and objectives and also of defining opportunity. Only 50 percent, however, incorporate the other individual steps in the process methodology. Generally, we have found, the high number of "yes" answers for defining opportunity/assessing value creation reflects that companies are doing the former rather than the latter. Most companies do a fairly inadequate job of assessing value creation, and that leads to a lot of failed negotiations.

Exhibit 8.8. Successful Alliance Companies Are Better at Planning Integration and Assessing Leverage and Bargaining Power

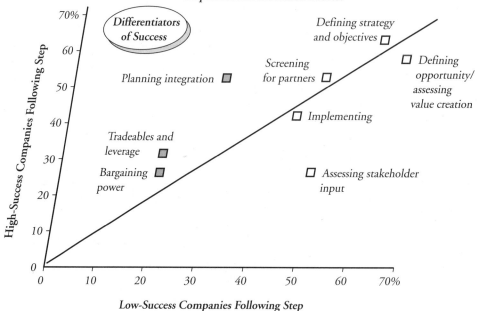

Steps Followed in Alliance Process

Source: Booz·Allen & Hamilton survey on institutionalizing alliance capabilities, 1997.

It is important to note that about half the companies use an alliance database, but few use it to capture lessons learned. Almost all the databases include a list of all active alliances with descriptions and the date formed, but very few present information in such areas as lessons learned. (Surprisingly, less than 20 percent of the companies using a database include alliance lessons learned.) The successful companies are slightly more likely to use a database, but the more significant differences are in the database materials. Successful companies are more likely to include lessons learned, key contacts, negotiations under way (so the company's executives can avoid stumbling into each other in potential partners' lobbies), and active and inactive alliances. In short, their databases are much richer in content than the databases the less successful companies use.

Another key activity in instilling institutional learning is doing self-assessments and asking one's partners for their opinions too. About two-thirds of the companies surveyed did self-assessments, but less than half asked their partners to assess how they were performing as partners (see Exhibit 8.9). This is a big area of potential improvement for all companies, as such feedback can be an important source of lessons learned and ideas on how to improve. The feedback can be substantive ("You are not staffing the right people in our venture") or less earth-shattering ("You do not keep us adequately informed," or, "You do not respond quickly enough to our phone calls"). Just as when your spouse complains about how annoying it is when you leave the cap off the toothpaste tube, even feedback about little things can defuse tensions and reduce patterns of disruptive behavior. As might be expected, successful alliance companies do more of both kinds of assessments and are twice as likely to do partner assessments as less successful companies.

Motorola recognized early how alliances could play an important role in its achieving its goals. After having been through a number of alliances, Motorola's management realized that having a disciplined process was the key to alliance success. One part of the Motorola process focuses on the selection of strategic partners. It starts with having a clear alliance strategy and objectives, which are linked to the overall corporate or business strategic objectives (see Exhibit 8.10). The next step screens for partners on such criteria as alliance experience and fit with value creation capabilities, along with the willingness of a potential partner to ally. For first-time partners, Motorola offers an alliance-training seminar that gives them information on Motorola's alliance requirements and process.

Exhibit 8.9. Fewer Than Half the Companies Ask Partners for Evaluations

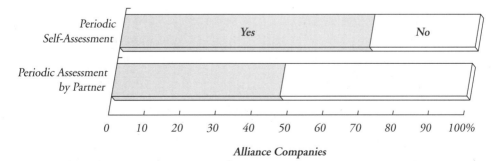

Source: Booz·Allen & Hamilton survey on institutionalizing alliance capabilities, 1997.

Exhibit 8.10.   Motorola Uses a Disciplined Approach to Finding Partners

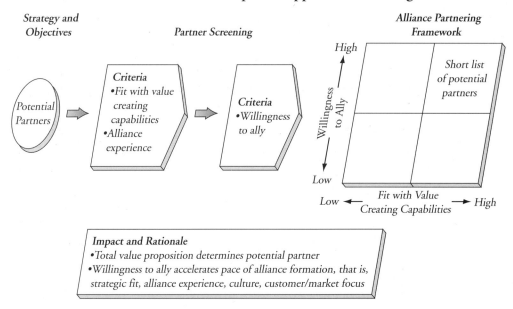

Using a best practice framework to develop a disciplined approach to alliance formation and to build an institutionalized alliance capability skill base has worked for many companies (the five ratings for best practice skill level are discussed in Chapter Five). One telecommunications company, for example, in an industry going through rapid, even convulsive, changes, saw alliances as a way to increase competitive strength and value creation for customers. However, senior management rated itself at Level 2, the second lowest skill level, for the best practice creatively planning to bridge management styles of partners. Fifty percent of the companies we surveyed were positioned even lower, at Level 1; only 20 percent were at Level 2. Yet this particular best practice was rated as the most important to achieving alliance success. This telecommunications company has set about building this capability in a disciplined manner.

Disseminating Best Practices

The most successful alliance companies have learned that merely teaching managers bureaucratic rules does not suffice. Disciplined approaches and channels are needed to disseminate best practice knowledge and experience (see Exhibit 8.11).

The three most popular dissemination channels are

- *Electronic networks.* Xerox's TPA website, for example, contains best practices, policies, and a list of internal and external alliance experts, and it is available to primary employees.
- *Periodic education seminars.* HP, for example, conducts fifty two-day seminars a year as a way of educating its top one thousand executives.
- *Repositories of alliance knowledge.* Among the companies creating these locations where managers can go to acquire alliance knowledge and assistance are Ford, IBM, and Dun & Bradstreet.

Note that these approaches are not either/or. Many companies are developing all three capabilities.

One of the most popular approaches to disseminating alliance knowledge is the website. Companies usually start in Phase 1 (see Exhibit 8.12), where the system is ad hoc, with only major alliances mentioned in a loose format. Once alliances are recognized as a major force in an industry, companies move into Phase 2. Now the website captures

Exhibit 8.11.   Best Practices Are Being Taught Through Multiple Channels

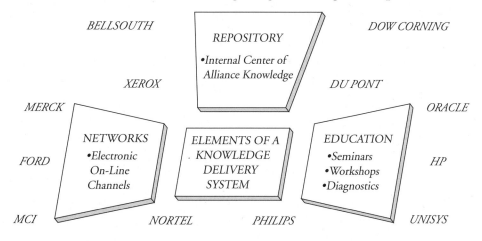

Exhibit 8.12. Websites of Alliance Knowledge Evolve

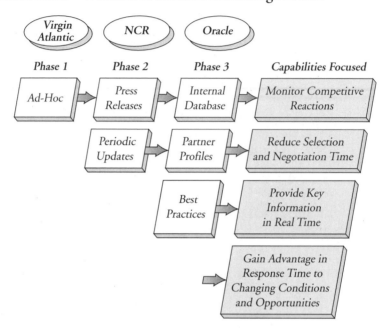

news announcements, and it is updated periodically and more formally maintained somewhere in the organization. As more and more alliances enter a company's portfolio, website capabilities expand rapidly, offering access to such elements as internal alliance and partner databases, partner profiles, and news announcements. A company's ability to monitor competitive reaction to its alliances, to reduce partner selection and negotiation time, and to provide key information is greatly enhanced by a website. Successful companies make better use of websites as alliance repositories. They are twice as likely to have an alliance website or a repository and the content is dramatically richer. This appears to be one of the biggest differentiators between successful and unsuccessful alliance companies.

Xerox's TPA and Booz·Allen's Knowledge on Line are examples of how companies use websites to transmit knowledge electronically (see Exhibit 8.13). Xerox and Booz·Allen decided a few years ago that knowledge available in real time can yield distinct competitive advantages. Xerox's TPA is positioned in the corporate alliance group. Similarly, Booz·Allen's KOL is managed by Booz·Allen's intellectual capital

Exhibit 8.13.   Electronic Knowledge Exchanges Can Offer Essential Information

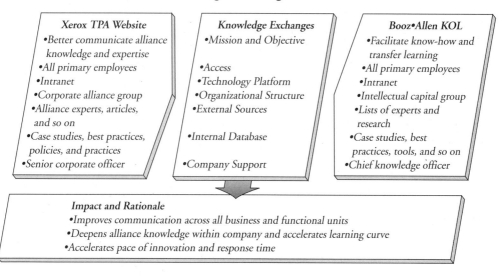

Xerox TPA Website
- *Better communicate alliance knowledge and expertise*
- *All primary employees*
- *Intranet*
- *Corporate alliance group*
- *Alliance experts, articles, and so on*
- *Case studies, best practices, policies, and practices*
- *Senior corporate officer*

Knowledge Exchanges
- *Mission and Objective*

- *Access*
- *Technology Platform*
- *Organizational Structure*
- *External Sources*

- *Internal Database*

- *Company Support*

Booz•Allen KOL
- *Facilitate know-how and transfer learning*
- *All primary employees*
- *Intranet*
- *Intellectual capital group*
- *Lists of experts and research*
- *Case studies, best practices, tools, and so on*
- *Chief knowledge officer*

Impact and Rationale
- *Improves communication across all business and functional units*
- *Deepens alliance knowledge within company and accelerates learning curve*
- *Accelerates pace of innovation and response time*

group and is available throughout the company. It contains case studies, best practices, presentations, and external and internal intellectual capital sources.

Emphasizing Training

Only one-third of the companies we surveyed offered alliance training and less than 15 percent had developed their own curriculum (see Exhibit 8.14). Successful alliance companies, however, recognize that alliances are fundamentally different from acquisitions and require special programs to bring managers up to speed.

BellSouth recognized the phenomenal growth of alliances in the telecommunications industry. After trying different training approaches, it decided to put 150 senior managers through an alliance workshop for two days, and it captured some intriguing lessons from this experience:

- People learn from each other.
- Seminar content must be specific to the company and industry (as was also seen at HP).
- Definitions and processes work.

Exhibit 8.14.   Only One-Third of Companies Offer Alliance Training

ALLIANCE TRAINING COURSES

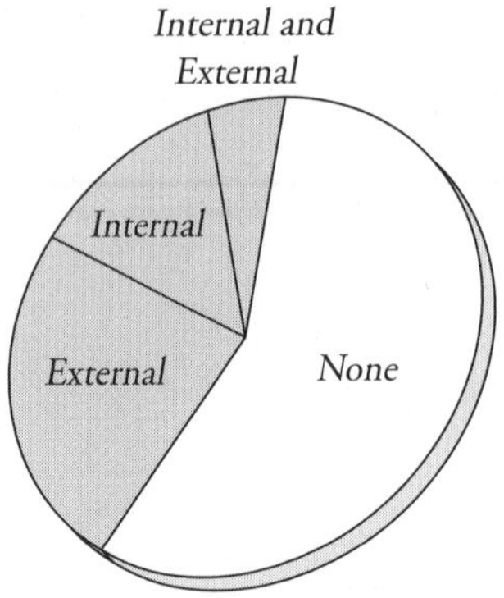

Internal and
External

Internal

External   None

Source: Booz·Allen & Hamilton survey on institutionalizing alliance capabilities, 1997.

Northern Telecom also decided, after one alliance failed, that train-ing should become part of its alliance program. It built a program on these three legs: organizational planning, three-day workshops, and network-ing. BellSouth and Northern Telecom are also learning by doing—disre-garding what does not work and embracing what does (see Exhibit 8.15).

Finding Organizational Solutions and Embedding

When we asked companies where their alliance functional resources re-side, we found that almost every imaginable model seems to exist. About a third of the companies lodged the resources on the corporate level, and about a quarter in the operating unit. The balance mixed the resources throughout the corporate and operating unit levels (see Exhibit 8.16). Successful alliance companies were more likely to have corporate func-tional groups. Almost 60 percent of successful companies have alliance functional groups only at the corporate level, compared with less than 40 percent of the less successful companies. Moreover, 95 percent of the successful companies have some alliance functional expertise *somewhere.* Finally, less successful companies are twice as likely to duplicate their al-liance functional expertise in the corporate and operating units.

Exhibit 8.15. Companies Build Alliance Training Engines

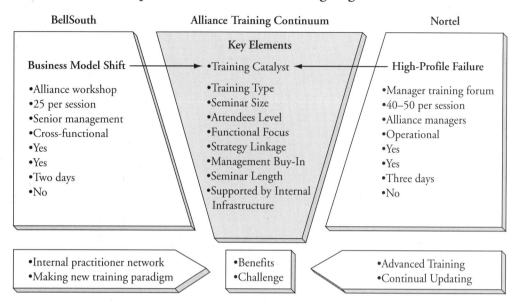

BellSouth	Alliance Training Continuum	Nortel
	Key Elements	
Business Model Shift	•Training Catalyst	**High-Profile Failure**
•Alliance workshop	•Training Type	•Manager training forum
•25 per session	•Seminar Size	•40–50 per session
•Senior management	•Attendees Level	•Alliance managers
•Cross-functional	•Functional Focus	•Operational
•Yes	•Strategy Linkage	•Yes
•Yes	•Management Buy-In	•Yes
•Two days	•Seminar Length	•Three days
•No	•Supported by Internal Infrastructure	•No

•Internal practitioner network	•Benefits	•Advanced Training
•Making new training paradigm	•Challenge	•Continual Updating

Source: Alliance Analyst, Aug. 19, 1996.

What these data suggest is that by placing alliance functional capability in both corporate and operating units, the less successful companies dilute their efforts, and less learning is captured and transferred. In terms of reporting relationships, we also saw that alliance reporting is moving into the executive suite.

Xerox has chosen the corporate route, creating a corporate group of relationship managers for key alliances such as Fuji Xerox. The job of a relationship manager is to coordinate across the alliance partners. This system offers both clear advantages and unique challenges (see Exhibit 8.17). Some companies, including HP, have embedded the alliance function within the business development group. Exhibit 8.17 also shows the advantages and challenges of this choice and of the method, adopted by other companies including Unisys, of placing alliance activity within each appropriate business unit.

In every case, the right structure is the one that meets your company's needs and objectives. Only value creation is important. Your decision needs to be clearly consistent with your company's culture and mode of decision making.

Exhibit 8.16.   Successful Alliance Companies Are Likely to Have Corporate Functional Alliance Groups

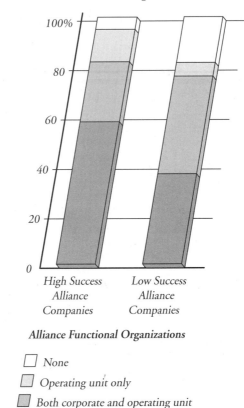

Alliance Functional Organizations

☐ None

▨ Operating unit only

▨ Both corporate and operating unit

▨ Corporate only

Source: Booz·Allen & Hamilton survey on institutionalizing alliance capabilities, 1997.

Implications for Management: Building Centers of Alliance Excellence

Global managers must question the adequacy of the way they do business today. A new language of cooperation has emerged. Many companies have already begun to position themselves in this new environment, but they need to raise the level of their game in the area of alliance execution by an order of magnitude. Otherwise, they will face a consortium of competitors experienced in alliance building yet have no experience in alliance building themselves.

Exhibit 8.17.   Companies Are Choosing Different Alliance Functional Group Solutions

Comparative Dimensions	Corporate Alliance Group (Xerox)	Business Development Group (HP)	Business Unit Alliance Groups (Unisys)
Characteristics	•Senior executive champion •Relationship managers •Defined tools and policies •Knowledge repository •Advisory council overseer •Assistance to SBUs •Coordination across alliance partners	•Report to business development •Clearinghouse for information •Best practice development •Monitoring of alliances •Exposure to finance expertise •Part of corporate •Seminars for executives	•Activity in SBUs •SBU manager reports to corporate advisory council •Alliances drive from SBU •Informal cross-SBU communication •No formal organization required
Advantages	•Knowledge/staff available to SBUs •Monitoring of key alliances	•Limited staff and broad view •Center of expertise	•Limited bureaucracy •Fast decision making
Challenges	•Not to be seen as no impact on value creation	•Conflict with mergers and acquisitions activity •No clear implementation power •Limited linkage to corporate strategy development	•Limited knowledge capture •Limited learning transfer •Limited cross-SBU leverage

Source: Alliance Analyst.

As we said early in this book, the important question is no longer, Should we form a strategic alliance? Now the questions are

- What types of arrangements are most appropriate?
- How do we successfully manage these alliances?
- What are we learning from the experiences of ourselves and others?

Judging from the numerous recently announced partnerships, an increasing number of global enterprises recognize that strategic alliances can provide growth at a fraction of the cost of going it alone. In addition to sharing risks and investment, a well-structured, well-managed approach to alliance formation can support other goals, such as efficiency and productivity. Alliances open the way for organizations to leverage resources.

To companies struggling with the appropriate role of alliances in a globalizing industry, we would say that your struggle is not unique and that we have observed many different organizational models (see Exhibit 8.18). In many cases, these models are evolutionary, as companies

Exhibit 8.18. The Model for Global Organizations Evolves

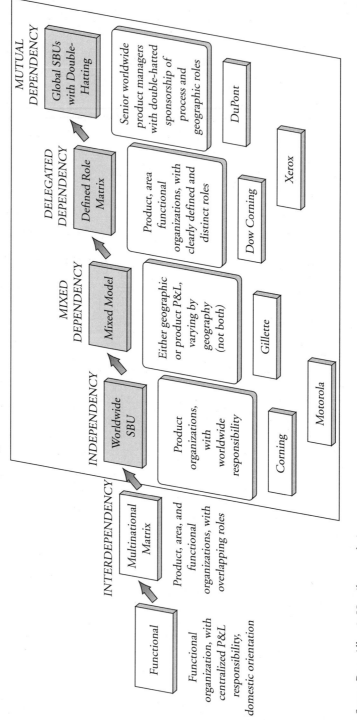

Source: Booz-Allen & Hamilton analysis.

grow from the models on the left in Exhibit 8.18 to the models on the right. Most organizations start with a model arranged around business functions and move eventually into some sort of matrix model with overlapping functional, product, and area organizations. Although this kind of interdependence can at least get issues (like alliances) on the table, it tends to fall apart, a victim of its own weight.

The next stage is a corporate strategic business unit model, where the product dimension gains supremacy and reduces overall cost by eliminating the overlaps across geographic regions. The last three models use various methods of mutual dependency and interdependency to ensure that the appropriate trade-offs are being made. The mixed-role model is managed by geographic dimension in some areas of the world and by product line dimension in others. Gillette is one example of such a company.

The defined role model has different elements of the matrix responsible for different organizational aspects, but it is clear who has control of any single aspect. Dow Corning is an example of this model. Most advanced in evolution is the global SBU model, with one executive in each area both holding area responsibility and providing functional leadership, a so-called double-hatted role. DuPont is an example. The mutual dependency in this model keeps everyone in a mode of trying to be supportive of and helpful to each other within the leadership team. It also avoids the power struggles inherent in a model where the geographic dimension has a different set of managers than the product line dimension.

As the new emphasis on capability access blurs industry lines and expands markets globally, defining new competitive arenas, the benefits companies once gained from industry position are not enough, and new capabilities are required to succeed. The name of the game is to maximize delivered value, to minimize total cost, and to gain competitive advantage. To meet this challenge and take advantage of the many ways alliances can help them play this game, successful alliance makers are beginning to establish *centers of alliance excellence* (see Exhibit 8.19).

Sophisticated alliance companies quickly observe that alliance learning yields big results. As we have illustrated, to capture this learning and transfer it to key employees, these companies are building best practice

Exhibit 8.19.   Successful Alliance Makers Are Establishing Centers of Excellence

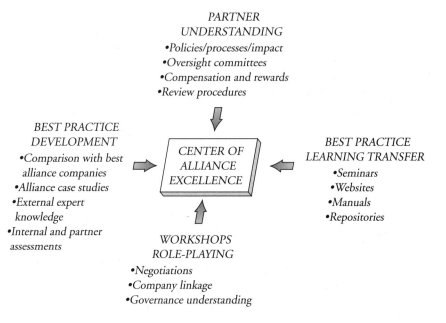

databases augmented by case studies and external expertise, incorporating their partners' assessment into the process, developing learning transfer channels and holding workshops, and developing role-playing programs. As companies depend more on alliances as engines for growth, we expect to see more and more resources devoted to creating such centers of excellence.

The Authors

John R. Harbison is a vice president with Booz·Allen & Hamilton Inc. He leads Booz·Allen's strategic alliances functional practice, global aerospace practice, Los Angeles office, and has recently served as a member of the board of directors and as chairman of the finance committee. In his eighteen years at Booz·Allen, Harbison has led over two hundred strategy engagements in more than thirty industries. In recent years he has led Booz·Allen's functional competency centers in strategic alliances and postmerger integration and has authored or coauthored *Viewpoint*s on related subjects, including such titles as *Post-Merger Integration: Capturing Value after the Deal* (1988); *A Practical Guide to Strategic Alliances: Leapfrogging the Learning Curve* (1994); *Cross-Border Alliances in the Age of Collaboration* (1997); *Institutionalizing Alliance Skills: Secrets of Repeatable Success* (1997); and *Strategic Management: Dinosaur or Differentiator?* (1997). He has led scores of client engagements, assisting companies in the formation and implementation of external alliances and acquisitions.

Harbison and his teams have received four nominations for the Booz·Allen Professional Excellence Award—given each year for the two engagements with greatest distinction in terms of client value created and intellectual capital formed—and two of those teams have won the award. He has authored articles and been quoted in dozens of major international publications. He has appeared on network news broadcasts on ABC, CNN, CBS (*Sixty Minutes*), Bloomberg, CNBC, and PBS (*McNeil-Lehrer NewsHour*). He has been quoted extensively in the *Alliance Analyst* (the premiere publication on the subject of strategic alliances) and now serves on the advisory board of that publication. He is also a frequent speaker at conferences, on topics such as strategic alliances and strategic management.

Prior to joining Booz·Allen, Harbison served as a senior accountant with Peat Marwick Mitchell. He holds a B.A. degree cum laude in English from Harvard College and an M.B.A. degree with first-year honors from Harvard Business School.

Peter Pekar Jr. is a recognized expert in strategic alliances. His familiarity with the alliance phenomenon comes not only from an academic and consulting perspective but also from hands-on experience as the operating manager of many alliances and responsible for their success. Since 1993, Pekar has been a senior adviser to Booz·Allen & Hamilton in the area of strategic alliances. His work covers numerous world-class client assignments and research in the United States, Asia, Europe, and Latin America. Pekar is also a visiting professor at the London Business School. He teaches a course on strategic alliances for M.B.A. students and holds alliance seminars for senior executives.

Pekar has been a guest speaker for such organizations and groups as Business Week's President's Forum; the Conference Board; National Association of Corporate Directors; Association for Corporate Growth; the Los Angeles and Chicago Bar Associations; Booz·Allen's senior advisory board, which Henry Kissinger chairs; and Stanford, Chicago, Northwestern, and Columbia Universities, and other schools.

Pekar has published over fifty articles and coauthored (with John Harbison) four *Viewpoints* on strategic alliances and strategic management, which have been distributed to over 30,000 senior global executives by Booz·Allen, to over 5,500 corporate directors by the National Association of Corporate Directors, and to over 3,000 subscribers of the *Alliance Analyst* by that newsletter's editors. He consults and holds seminars and training sessions for many corporations.

Pekar's business career spans more than two decades. Before coming to Booz·Allen, he was president of BT-U.S.A. Inc., a $600 million U.S. holding company for a global Dutch conglomerate. Prior to that, he was head of alliances and venture capital for Dun & Bradstreet. He also has held senior management positions in such Fortune 500 firms as Esmark and Quaker Oats. He holds an M.A. degree in mathematics from the University of Illinois (Urbana) and a Ph.D. degree in business and economics from the Illinois Institute of Technology's Stuart School of Business.

Index

Booz·Allen & Hamilton

Booz·Allen & Hamilton is one of the world's leading international management and technology consulting firms, providing services in strategy, systems, operations, and technology to clients in more than seventy-five countries around the globe.

Founded in 1914, Booz·Allen & Hamilton pioneered the business of management consulting. Today, Booz·Allen has more than eight thousand employees in ninety offices on six continents and revenues of $1.4 billion. Its clients comprise a majority of the world's largest industrial and service corporations, as well as major institutions and government bodies around the world, including most U.S. federal departments and agencies.

Booz·Allen is a private corporation organized into two major business sectors: the Worldwide Commercial Business (WCB) and the Worldwide Technology Business (WTB). WCB clients are primarily major international corporations; WTB generally serves governmental clients both in the United States and abroad.

Booz·Allen helps senior management solve complex problems through its expertise in more than two dozen industries as well as information technology, operations management, and strategic leadership.

Consistent with its position as a business thought leader, Booz·Allen publishes the award-winning quarterly journal, *Strategy & Business,* which reports on the latest developments in global management techniques, competitive tactics, and strategic thinking.

Booz·Allen & Hamilton is a founding cosponsor of the annual Global Business Book Awards. GBBA recognizes the most innovative contributions to business literature and promotes worldwide readership of business books.

For more information, please visit Booz·Allen's Website at www.bah.com. Or contact the company at:

Booz·Allen & Hamilton
101 Park Ave.
New York, NY 10178
(212) 697–1900

This *Strategy & Business* book is an excellent business relationship-building tool. By giving this book to your clients, partners, and prospects, you can contribute to their knowledge in a business world where staying current is the only lasting competitive edge. Receive substantial quantity discounts when you place bulk orders. Let us personalize the books with your message.

For quantity discounts and customized orders, contact:

Bernadette Walter
Corporate Sales Manager
Jossey-Bass Publishers
350 Sansome Street
San Francisco, CA 94104–1342
phone: (415) 782–3122
fax: (415) 433–0499
e-mail: bwalter@jbp.com